Except For Fornication

Why Evangelicals Must Reevaluate Their Interpretation
Of Matthew's Divorce Exception Clause

Daniel R. Jennings

SEAN
MULTIMEDIA
www.seanmultimedia.com

Except For Fornication

Copyright © 2011 by Daniel R. Jennings

ISBN-13: 978-1475095395 ISBN-10:1475095392

Jennings, Daniel, R. 1977-
    Except For Fornication.

Special thanks to Dr. Vic Reasoner and Casey Whitaker for their review of the pre-publication manuscript.

οτι ουκ αδυνατησει παρα του θεου παν ρημα

Lucas I.XXXVII

TABLE OF CONTENTS

Is It Post-Marital Adultery Or Pre-Marital Fornication That Justifies Divorce And Remarriage?

For nearly five hundred years Protestant scholars have been debating the meaning of Jesus' teachings on divorce and remarriage in Matthew 19:9a. The debate centers on the best way to translate one word in that verse which determines the meaning of the entire passage. That word is *porneia* and, as the following two popular translations will show, how it is translated makes all the difference in one's understanding of this passage.

King James Version	New International Version
And I say unto you, Whosoever shall put away his wife, except it be for <u>fornication</u> (*porneia*), and shall marry another, committeth adultery:	I tell you that anyone who divorces his wife, except for <u>marital unfaithfulness</u> (*porneia*), and marries another woman commits adultery.

The difference in opinion as to what the underlying Greek word *porneia* means has led to two differing interpretations of this passage:

1.) The Fornication View, reflected in the King James Version's translation of this passage, which holds that if a man discovers that his wife has had sexual relations with someone else *before* they were married (i.e. committed fornication) then he is justified in divorcing and remarrying.

2.) The Adultery View, reflected in the New International Version's translation, which holds that if a man's wife has had sexual relations *after* they are married (i.e. committed adultery) then he is justified in divorcing her and remarrying.

The **Fornication View** holds that the underlying Greek word, prior to and at the time of Jesus, was used generally to refer to sexual behavior by single persons (i.e. fornication).

The **Adultery View** holds that this word was a catch-all phrase for sexual immorality in general prior to and at the time of Jesus and that in this context it is referring to adultery.

One's understanding of what this Greek word means will influence one's decision in how to translate it, and ultimately will influence one's teaching on who may remarry after divorce and under what circumstances.

It is important to understand this for a number of reasons. First, with the large increase in American divorces and remarriages since the 1970's, pastors need to understand what the New Testament teaches on this issue. And secondly, because Jesus indicated that even those who sin in ignorance will still be punished (Lk 12:47-48) it is of the utmost importance that persons contemplating remarrying after a divorce fully understand who can and cannot enter into a new marriage.

The purpose of this book is to explore the reasons that led me after several years of preaching the **Adultery View** to abandon it in favor of the **Fornication View**. As a younger Christian I held very strongly to the **Adultery View** but this was not because I had sat down and tried to formulate a theology of divorce and remarriage. I had simply been raised to believe this view and when I began taking undergraduate theological training this was the only view presented by my professors. I did not really sit down and conclude that the **Adultery View** was the correct interpretation (I did not even know that there was another interpretation for many years), I was just taught this from my youth and never really looked into it much further. It was only after graduating from Bible College and studying historical theology that I realized that there was an alternative view and I would like to present in this book some of the reasons that led me to change my views and accept the **Fornication View**.

These reasons included the facts that the way pre-New Testament, New Testament and post-New Testament writers used the *porneia* family of words lent more credence to the Fornication View than it did to the Adultery View; the King James translation committee and numerous other translations have favored the Fornication View; the Adultery View causes Matthew 19:9a to contradict Luke 16:18 which deals with an adulterous spouse; the Fornication View matches an actual reference to concealed pre-nuptial sin in the Law of Moses; there is a theological explanation for the Fornication View based upon the idea of covenant; the Fornication View is found in natural law; there are logical answers to the common objections that are raised against the Fornication View; the Adultery View has been rejected by Christians throughout history; and the clear teachings of the New Testament upon divorce and remarriage do not leave any room for an adultery exception.

A Simple Grammar Lesson To
Understand The Porneia Family Of Words

Before going any further we need to become a little more familiar with the word *porneia* and this can be accomplished by doing a simple English grammar lesson with the word "robbery".

In English *robbery* is a noun that describes the act of robbing someone. The word used to describe the person who performs the robbery is *robber* and this is also a noun. A verb is used to describe the word that is used to reflect the actual action of the person who commits the robbery and one form of that word would be *robbing*. So in this case we have three different categories of the same word:

Nouns		Verb
The Act Of Robbery	**The Person Who Performs The Robbery**	**The Actual Action Of Performing Robbery**
Robbery	Robber	Robbing

Now it is the same way with the Greek family of words related to *porneia*, two groups of nouns and a verb group:

Nouns			Verb
The Act Of Porneia	**The Person Who Performs The Porneia**		**The Actual Action Of Performing Porneia**
Porneia	Porneion Pornikos Pornokopos	Porne Pornos	Porneuo Ek-porneuo Kata-porneuo

To make this a little simpler we can use the English word "fornication", which has been used by many translations to translate *porneia*, to better illustrate this.

Noun	Noun	Verb
The Act Of Fornication	**The Person Who Performs The Fornication**	**The Actual Action Of Performing Fornication**
Fornication	Fornicator	Fornicating

Now that we have established these basic rules of grammar for *porneia* we are in a better position to examine how Greek literature (both before and after the time of the New Testament) used this family of words.

The Way Pre-New Testament Writers Used Porneia

One of the factors that contributed to my abandoning the Adultery View in favor of the Fornication View was the way that Greek literature written prior to the New Testament used the *porneia* family of words. While it is rare in pre-New Testament literature one thing that did stick out to me about its usage in those writings was that it was generally used to refer to *sexual behavior by single people* who were committing fornication either for pleasure or for pay (prostitution). Aeschines (389-314BC) and Demosthenes (384–322BC) used it to refer to the behavior of a man who had been a reputed prostitute in his youth *as a single man.*[1]

---

[1] "For he says that when I was prosecuting Timarchus I said that his **porneia** was a matter of common report…" (Aeschines, *On the Embassy 2:144* [Charles Darwin Adams, tr.])

"…he is guilty of selling his person not only in Misgolas' house, but in the house of another man also, and again of another, and that from this last he went to still another, surely you will no longer look upon him as one who has merely been a kept man, but— by Dionysus, I don't know how I can keep glossing the thing over all day long—as a common **porneuo**. For the man who follows these practices recklessly and with many men and for pay seems to me to be chargeable with precisely this." (Aeschines, *Against Timarchus, 52* [Ibid.])

"When, therefore, I have dared to bring impeachment against Timarchus for having **porneuo** himself…" (Aeschines, *Against Timarchus, 119* [Ibid.])

"For he is amazed, he says, if you do not all remember that every single year the senate farms out the tax on **pornikos** (prostitutes), and that the men who buy this tax do not guess, but know precisely, who they are that follow this profession." (Aeschines, *Against Timarchus, 119* [Ibid.])

"And then the assurance of the man! Bringing another man before this court on a charge of **porneia**! However, I will let that go for the present." (Demosthenes, *Speech 19: On The Embassy, 200* [C. A. Vince and J. H. Vince, tr.])

"But that was nothing: under his eyes sat his brother Aphobetus. In truth, on that day all that declaiming against **porneia** was like water flowing upstream." (Demosthenes, *Speech 19: On The Embassy, 287* [Ibid.])

Herodotus (c.484–c.425BC) used it to refer to *single women* who sell themselves sexually in order to raise enough money to get married.[2] The Greek translation of the Old Testament (300-200BC) used it to describe the behavior of Tamar, the *single widow* who tricked her former father-in-law Judas (also a *single widower*[3]) to have sex with her;[4] the behavior of Dinah a *single, never married* woman who has intercourse with the Hivite prince Shechem;[5] and a bride who secretly had sexual intercourse before marriage with a man other than her future husband and hid it from her husband-to-be.[6] The Apocryphal book of Sirach (1st Cent. BC) used it to refer to sexual behavior by *individuals who are still under their parents care*.[7] Finally, Strabo (c.54BC-25AD) used it to describe the custom of parents

---

For full details on the immoral life of this individual see Aeschine's *Against Timarchus*, 39-100.

[2] "For the daughters of the common people in Lydia practice **porneuo** one and all, to gather for themselves dowries, continuing this until the time when they marry; and the girls give themselves away in marriage." (*Histories 1:93* [G. C. Macaulay, tr.])

"Now the Lydians have very nearly the same customs as the Hellenes, with the exception that they **kata-porneuo** (prostitute) their female children…" (*Histories 1:94* [Ibid.])

[3] Gen 38:12

[4] Your daughter-in-law Thamar has **played the whore** (*ek-porneuo*), and see, she is with child by **whoredom** (*porneia*). Gen 38:24NETS

[5] "And Deina the daughter of Leia, whom she bore to Jacob, went out to make an acquaintance with the daughters of the neighbours. And Sychem the son of Emmor the Evite, who was the prince of the country, saw her and took her and lay with her and humbled her…And they (Simeon and Levi) said, But shall they treat our sister like a **harlot** (*porne*)?" (Gen 34:1-2, 31Thomson)

[6] "And if any one should take a wife, and dwell with her, and hate her, and attach to her reproachful words, and bring against her an evil name, and say, I took this woman, and when I came to her I found not her tokens of virginity: then the father and the mother of the damsel shall take and bring out the damsel's tokens of virginity to the elders of the city to the gate…But if this report be true, and the tokens of virginity be not found for the damsel; then shall they bring out the damsel to the doors of her father's house, and shall stone her with stones, and she shall die; because she has wrought folly among the children of Israel, to defile the house of her father by **whoring** (*ek-porneuo*): so thou shalt remove the evil one from among you." (Dt 22:13-21Brenton)

[7] "Be ashamed of **whoredom** (*porneia*) before father and mother: and of a lie before a prince and a mighty man …" (Sirach 41:17KJV)

who took their *young, unmarried daughters* and consecrated them to a life of prostitution in the temple of a goddess.[8]

The pre-New Testament usage is rare and not entirely clear but as we move into the New Testament era and beyond the evidence becomes much more compelling for the Fornication View.

The Way New Testament Writers Used Porneia

Another factor that strongly contributed to the changing of my mind about the Adultery View was examining how New Testament writers used this word in relation to adultery.

In New Testament Greek there is another Greek word which specifically means "adultery" and it is the word *moichao*. It is part of a family of words, all of which mean and were used to convey the idea of *post-marital unfaithfulness*.[9] Interestingly, it is actually used in Matthew 19:9a alongside of *porneia* when Jesus says, "whoever shall put away his wife, except it be for fornication (*porneia*), and shall marry another, commits adultery (*moichao*)". If Matthew's Gospel had been trying to tell us that adultery was a justifiable reason for divorce and remarriage then I did not understand why he did not simply use the common Greek word for adultery. That would have helped to end the debate right there.

Several hundred years before Matthew wrote his Gospel the Old Testament was translated into Greek and this translation is referred to as the Septuagint. If the writer of Matthew's Gospel had wanted to present the idea that adultery was the sin that justified divorce and remarriage in Matthew 19:9a then it seems very likely that he would have used the same Greek word which the Septuagint translators used to translate the seventh commandment: *Thou shalt not commit adultery* (Ex 20:13). Yet, interestingly, the translators of the Septuagint did not use *porneia* to translate Exodus 20:13 but one of the common Greek words for

---

[8] "This, indeed, is not a remarkable thing; but the most illustrious men of the tribe actually consecrate to her their daughters while maidens; and it is the custom for these first to be **kata-porneuo** (prostituted) in the temple of the goddess for a long time and after this to be given in marriage; and no one disdains to live in wedlock with such a woman." (*Geography*, 11.14.16 [H. L. Jones, tr.])

[9] Other members of this word family include *moichalis*, *moicheia*, *moicheuo*, and *moichos*.

adultery.[10] If Matthew's Gospel was trying to tell us that "adultery" was the only acceptable reason for divorcing and remarrying it is very unclear as to why he did not use the commonly accepted word which so clearly meant adultery that it was used in the Greek version of the Ten Commandments and of which every Greek speaking Jew would immediately understand to refer to adultery. In fact, the Septuagint never once uses the *porneia* family of words to translate any of the three Hebrew words for adultery.[11] These words appear 34 times in the Hebrew Old Testament and in none of these cases was the word *porneia* chosen by the Septuagint translators to translate any of them.

A second clue from the New Testament usage of *porneia* is its usage alongside of adultery in other New Testament passages. If *porneia* carried with it the idea of committing adultery we would not expect to see it used alongside of the *moichao* family of words but instead we see just the opposite. We see that when the New Testament writers list sins they include *porneia* along with the *moichao* family of words which implies that they did not understand *porneia* to mean adultery. Consider the following:

> **For out of the heart proceed evil thoughts, murders, adulteries (*moicheia*), fornications (*porneia*), thefts, false witness, blasphemies... Mt 15:19**

> **For from within, out of the heart of men, proceed evil thoughts, adulteries (*moicheia*), fornications (*porneia*), murders... Mk 7:21**

> **Now the works of the flesh are manifest, which are these; Adultery (*moicheia*), fornication (*porneia*), uncleanness, lasciviousness... Ga 5:19**

> **Do you not know that the unrighteous will not inherit the kingdom of God? Do not deceived: neither fornicators (*pornos*), nor idolaters, nor adulterers (*moichos*), nor effeminate, nor abusers of themselves with mankind... 1Co 6:9**

---

[10] The word *moicheuo*.

[11] The Hebrew words are *na'aph* (Strong's H5003), *ni'uph* (H5004), and *na'aphuwph* (H5005).

Marriage is honorable among all, and the bed undefiled: but fornicators (*pornos*) and adulterers (*moichos*) God will judge. He 13:4NKJV

If *porneia* carried with it the idea of adultery at the time the New Testament was written then the above writers would not have included the Greek word for adultery in their lists of sins along with *porneia*. It wouldn't have made sense to do so. It should be obvious that when Matthew, Mark, Paul and the anonymous author of Hebrews were writing their lists of sins above that when it came to the use of the word *porneia* that they were so sure that their readers would not understand it to mean adultery that they made sure that they specifically listed the Greek word for adultery along with *porneia*. If they had understood *porneia* to carry with it the idea of "adultery *and* fornication" then they would have only put it and left out *moichao* knowing that their readers would understand the one word to mean *both* sins. But they chose not to. If *porneia* carried with it the idea of *adultery and fornication* then there would have been no need or reason for the writers to include the Greek word for adultery along with *porneia*. Instead of using two words which meant the same thing they would have only used *porneia*. It seems clear that Matthew, Mark, Paul and the author of Hebrews all understood that the people who committed *porneia* and the people who committed *adultery* were two different groups of people. To illustrate this further consider the following sentences:

"My pet is a dog and a canine."

"I have a sickness and an illness."

"He is a man and a male."

No one would talk or write like that. It doesn't make sense to do so. The writers of the New Testament would not have put both *porneia* and *moichao* together in the same sentence if they meant the same thing. The New Testament evidence strongly suggests that *porneia* in the first century did not mean adultery.

8

The Way Post-New Testament Writers Used Porneia

Another factor that led to me rejecting the Adultery View in favor of the Fornication View was the way that Greek literature *after* the time of the New Testament used the *porneia* family of words. After doing an in-depth study of how Greek writers from the 1st to the 5th centuries used *porneia* it became clear to me that Greek writers after the time of the New Testament generally understood *porneia* and adultery to be *two different* things as the following sixty post-New Testament quotations from Greek literature demonstrate.[12]

The Teaching Of The Twelve Apostles (a.k.a. The Didache) (1st-2nd Cent.):

"And the second commandment of the Teaching; Thou shalt not commit murder, thou shalt not commit **adultery** (*moicheuo*), thou shalt not commit paederasty, thou shalt not commit **fornication** (*porneuo*), thou shalt not steal, thou shalt not practice magic..." (*Ch. 2/Charles Taylor*[13])

"And the way of death is this: First of all it is evil and full of curse: murders, **adulteries** (*moicheia*), lusts, **fornications** (*porneia*), thefts, idolatries, magic arts, witchcrafts, rapines, false witnessings, hypocrisies, double-heartedness, deceit, haughtiness, depravity, self-will, greediness, filthy talking, jealousy, over-confidence, loftiness, boastfulness..." (*Ch. 5/Charles Taylor*[14])

Barnabas (c.130AD):

"Thou shalt not commit **fornication** (*porneuo*): thou shalt not commit **adultery** (*moicheuo*): thou shalt not be a corrupter of youth." (*Epistle, Ch. 19/PG 2:777*)

---

[12] Unless otherwise indicated all English translations in the Post-New Testament Usage section are from the Ante-Nicene (Roberts & Donaldson, eds.) & Nicene & Post-Nicene Fathers (Schaff, ed.) series. The source of the Greek text used will be indicated at the end of the quote. In most case J.P. Migne's *Patrologia Graeca* (PG) was used as the Greek reference text.

[13] Greek text as it is found in Charles Taylor's *An Essay On The Theology Of The Didache, With The Greek Text: Forming An Appendix To Two lectures On The Teaching Of The Twelve Apostles* (Cambridge: Deighton Bell & Co., 1889), p.140.

[14] Ibid, p.142.

Justin Martyr (c.100-c.165AD):

"And when Urbicus ordered him to be led away to punishment, one Lucius, who was also himself a Christian, seeing the unreasonable judgment that had thus been given, said to Urbicus: "What is the ground of this judgment? Why have you punished this man, not as an **adulterer** (*moichos*), nor **fornicator** (*pornos*), nor murderer, nor thief, nor robber, nor convicted of any crime at all..." (*Second Apology, 2/ PG 6:445*)

"And I say nothing of the masculine character of Minerva, nor of the feminine nature of Bacchus, nor of the **fornicating** (*pornichon*) disposition of Venus. Read to Jupiter, ye Greeks, the law against parricides, and the penalty of **adultery** (*moicheia*), and the ignominy of paederasty." (*Discourse To The Greeks, 2/ PG 6:233*)

"For [God] sets before every race of mankind that which is always and universally just, as well as all righteousness; and every race knows that **adultery** (*moicheia*), and **fornication** (*porneia*), and homicide, and such like, are sinful..." (*Dialogue With Trypho, Ch 93/ PG 6:697*)

Hermas (160AD):

"What, sir," say I, "are the evil deeds from which we must restrain ourselves?" "Hear," says he: "from **adultery** (*moicheia*) and **fornication** (*porneia*), from unlawful reveling, from wicked luxury, from indulgence in many kinds of food and the extravagance of riches..." (*The Shepherd, Book 2, Commandment 8:3/Kirsopp Lake[15]*)

Aristides (2nd Cent.):

"They do not commit **adultery** (*moicheuo*) nor **fornication** (*porneuo*), nor bear false witness, nor covet the things of others; they honor father and mother..." (*Apology, 15/James Rendell Harris[16]*)

Theophilus (Late 2nd Cent.):

---

[15] Greek text from Kirsopp Lake's *The Apostolic Fathers With An English Translation, Vol. 2: The Shepherd Of Hermas, The Martyrdom Of Polycarp, & The Epistle To Diognetus* (London: William Heinemann, 1917), p. 102.

[16] Greek text from James Rendel Harris & Joseph Armitage Robinson, eds., *The Apology Of Aristides On Behalf Of The Christians, From A Syriac Ms. Preserved On Mount Sinai, Volume 1, Issue 1 Of Texts And Studies* (Cambridge: University Press, 1891), p.111.

"Do you, therefore, show me yourself, whether you are not an **adulterer** (*moichos*), or a **fornicator** (*pornos*), or a thief, or a robber, or a purloiner…" (*To Autolycus, 1:2/ PG 6:1028*)

"But to the unbelieving and despisers, who obey not the truth, but are obedient to unrighteousness, when they shall have been filled with **adulteries** (*moicheia*) and **fornications** (*porneia*), and filthiness, and covetousness, and unlawful idolatries, there shall be anger and wrath, tribulation and anguish…" (*To Autolycus, 1:14/ PG 6:1045*)

"And they also taught us to refrain from unlawful idolatry, and **adultery** (*moicheia*), and murder, **fornication** (*porneia*), theft, avarice, false swearing, wrath, and every incontinence and uncleanness…" (*To Autolycus, 2:34/ PG 6:1108*)

"Did they not, when they essayed to write even of honorable conduct, teach the perpetration of lasciviousness, and **fornication** (*porneia*), and **adultery** (*moicheia*); and did they not introduce hateful and unutterable wickedness?" (*To Autolycus, 3:3/ PG 6:1124*)

Testament Of The Twelve Patriarchs (192AD):

"Another committeth **adultery** (*moicheuo*) and **fornication** (*porneuo*), and abstaineth from meats; yet in his fasting he worketh evil, and by his power and his wealth perverteth many…" (*10:2, The Testimony Of Asher, Sec. 2/ PG 2:1121*)

Clement Of Alexandria (d.c.215AD):

"For he will not find the image of God dwelling within, as is meet; but instead of it a **fornicator** (*porne*) and **adulteress** (*moichalis*) has occupied the shrine of the soul." (*The Instructor, 3:2/ PG 8:561*)

"Thief, dost thou wish to get forgiveness? Steal no more. **Adulterer** (*moicheuo*), burn no more. **Fornicator** (*porneuo*), live for the future chastely." (*Who Is The Rich Man That Shall Be Saved, 40/ PG 9:645*)

Acts Of The Holy Apostle Thomas (Early 3rd Cent.):

"…and even if they be in good health, they will be again good-for-nothing, doing unprofitable and abominable works: for they will be detected either in **adultery** (*moicheia*), or in murder, or in theft, or in fornication (*porneia*), and by all these you will be afflicted. (*Constantin von Tischendorf*[17])

Hippolytus (d.c.236AD):

"To those, then, that have been orally instructed by him, he dispenses baptism in this manner, addressing to his dupes some such words as the following: 'If, therefore, (my) children, one shall have intercourse with any sort of animal whatsoever, or a male, or a sister, or a daughter, or hath committed **adultery** (*moicheuo*), or been guilty of **fornication** (*porneuo*), and is desirous of obtaining remission of sins…'" (*Refutation Of All Heresies, 9:10/ PG 16-3:3390*)

"But why, O prophet, tell us, and for what reason, was the temple made desolate? Was it on account of that ancient fabrication of the calf? Was it on account of the idolatry of the people? Was it for the blood of the prophets? Was it for the **adultery** (*moicheia*) and **fornication** (*porneia*) of Israel? By no means, he says; for in all these transgressions they always found pardon open to them…" (*Expository Treatise Against The Jews, 7/ PG 10:792*)

Origen:

"Next to this let us see how the things which proceed out and defile the man do not defile the man because of their proceeding out of the mouth, but have the cause of their defilement in the heart, when there come forth out of it, before those things which proceed through the mouth, evil thoughts, of which the species are — murders, **adulteries** (*moicheia*), **fornications** (*porneia*), thefts, false witness, railings." (*Commentary On Matthew, 11:15/ PG 13:952*)

"But observe here that every great sin is a loss of the talents of the master of the house, and such sins are committed by **fornicators** (*pornos*), **adulterers** (*moichos*), abusers of themselves with men, effeminate, idolaters, murderers." (*Commentary On The Gospel Of Matthew, Book 14:10/ PG 13:1208*)

Methodius (d.c.311AD):

---

[17] Greek text from Constantin von Tischendorf's *Acta Apostolorum Apocrypha* (Lipsiae: Avenarius & Mendelssohn, 1851), p.200.

"Consider now the fiery and bitter horn of **fornication** (*porneia*), by which he casts down the incontinent; consider **adultery** (*moicheia*), consider falsehood, covetousness, theft, and the other sister and related vices..." (*The Banquet Of The Ten Virgins, Discourse 8:13/ PG 18:160*)

Council Of NeoCaesarea (315AD):

"If a presbyter marry, let him be removed from his order; but if he commit **fornication** (*porneuo*) or **adultery** (*moicheuo*), let him be altogether cast out and put to penance." (*Canon 1/ Karl Joseph von Hefele*[18])

Athanasius (c.296-373):

"For from Zeus they have learned corruption of youth and **adultery** (*moicheia*), from Aphrodite **fornication** (*porneia*), from Rhea licentiousness, from Ares murders, and from other gods other like things..." (*Against The Heathen, 1:26:2/ PG 25:52*)

Cyril Of Jerusalem (c.315-386):

"Remember the Judgment, and neither **fornication** (*porneia*), nor **adultery** (*moicheia*), nor murder, nor any transgression of the law shall prevail with thee." (*Catechetical Lectures, 2:2/ PG 33:412*)

"It is he[19] that puts lusts into them that listen to him: from him come **adultery** (*moicheia*), **fornication** (*porneia*), and every kind of evil." (*Catechetical Lectures, Lecture 2:4/ PG 33:388*)

"For say not, I have committed **fornication** (*porneuo*) and **adultery** (*moicheuo*): I have done dreadful things, and not once only, but often: will He forgive?" (*Catechetical Lectures, 2:6/PG 33:413*)

"For all things whatsoever thou hast done shall be forgiven thee, whether it be **fornication** (*porneia*), or **adultery** (*moicheia*), or any other such form of licentiousness." (*Catechetical Lectures, 3:15/ PG 33:445*)

"But let all the other practices be banished afar, **fornication** (*porneia*), **adultery** (*moicheia*), and every kind of licentiousness: and let the body be kept pure for the Lord..." (*Catechetical Lectures, 4:26/ PG 33:489*)

---

[18] *A History Of The Councils Of The Church: To The Close Of The Council Of Nicea, A.D. 325.* William R. Clark, Tr. (Edinburgh: T&T Clark, 1871), p.223. The Greek text can also be found in Giovanni Domenico Mansi's *Sacrorum Conciliorum Nova Amplissima Collectio, 2:539.*

[19] That is, Satan.

Revelation Of Paul (4ᵗʰ Cent.):

"And he said to me: These are they who lived unrepenting in **fornications** (*porneia*) and **adulteries** (*moicheia*). (*Constantin von Tischendorf*[20])

Gregory Of Nyssa (d. after 386AD):

"Of those who fall into sin through desire and pleasure, this is the division: the one is called **adultery** (*moicheia*) and the other **fornication** (*porneia*)." (*Canonical Epistle To Letoius, Bishop Of Melitene, Canon 4a/ PG 45:228*)[21]

"**Fornication** (*porneia*) therefore is shown to be not far from the offence of **adultery** (*moicheia*) by those who look more accurately into its character, for the divine Scripture says, *do not be intimate with the stranger*." (*Canonical Epistle To Letoius, Bishop Of Melitene, Canon 4d/ PG 45:228*)[22]

"But since there has been some indulgence by the Fathers towards the weaker, the offence is therefore judged according to the generic division, with the result that any satisfaction of desire which occurs without injury to someone else is reckoned as **fornication** (*porneia*), whereas **adultery** (*moicheia*) is a plot and an injury against another." (*Canonical Epistle To Letoius, Bishop Of Melitene, Canon 4d/ PG 45:228*)[23]

Constitutions Of The Holy Apostles (4ᵗʰ Cent.):

"He is also to avoid **fornicators** (*pornos*), for "thou shall not offer the hire of an harlot to the Lord." He is also to avoid extortioners, and such as covet other men's goods, and **adulterers** (*moichos*); for the sacrifices of such as these are abominable with God." (*4:1:6/ PG 1:812*)

"Neither the burial of a man, nor a dead man's bone, nor a sepulcher, nor any particular sort of food, nor the nocturnal pollution, can defile the soul of man; but only impiety towards God, and transgression, and injustice

---

[20] Greek text from Constantin von Tischendorf & Justin Perkins' *Apocalypses Apocryphae: Mosis, Esdrae, Pauli, Iohannis, Item, Mariae Dormitio: Additis Evangeliorum Et Actuum Apocryphorum Supplementis* (Lipsiae: Herm. Mendelssohn, 1866), p.57.

[21] English text from Anna Silvas' *Gregory Of Nyssa: The Letters, Vol. 83 Of Supplements To Vigiliae Christianae* (Leiden: Brill, 2007).

[22] English text, ibid.

[23] English text, ibid.

towards one's neighbor; I mean rapine, violence, or if there be anything contrary to His righteousness, **adultery** (*moicheia*) or **fornication** (*porneia*)." (*6:5:27/ PG 1:981*)

"But **adultery** (*moicheia*) and **fornication** (*porneia*) are against the law; the one whereof is impiety, the other injustice, and, in a word, no other than a great sin. But neither sort of them is without its punishment in its own proper nature. For the practicers of one sort attempt the dissolution of the world, and endeavor to make the natural course of things to change for one that is unnatural; but those of the second sort — the adulterers — are unjust by corrupting others' marriages, and dividing into two what God hath made one, rendering the children suspected, and exposing the true husband to the snares of others." (*6:5:28/ PG 1:984*)

"But the way of death is known by its wicked practices: for therein is the ignorance of God, and the introduction of many evils, and disorders, and disturbances; whereby come murders, **adulteries** (*moicheia*), **fornications** (*porneia*), perjuries, unlawful lusts, thefts, idolatries, magic arts, witchcrafts, rapines, false-witnesses…" (*7:1:18/ PG 1:1009*)

Apostolic Canons (c.400AD):

"Canon 61: If there be an accusation against a Christian for **fornication** (*porneia*), or **adultery** (*moicheia*), or any other forbidden action, and he be convicted, let him not be promoted into the clergy." (*Apostolic Constitutions 8:5:47/ PG 137:160*)

Epiphanius of Salamis (d.403AD):

"For if an originator of evils is also an evildoer how can it not be found at once that God is good, as I have said in the other Sects, since he legislated against **fornication** (*porneia*), **adultery** (*moicheia*), rapine and covetousness?" (*Panarion, Heresy 40:7/ PG 41:689*)[24]

"Now the holy catholic church reveres virginity, the single life and purity, commends widowhood, and honors and accepts lawful wedlock; but it forbids **fornication** (*porneia*), **adultery** (*moicheia*) and unchastity." (*Panarion, Heresy 48:9/ PG 41:868*)

"And this means, 'not in **fornication** (*porneia*), **adultery** (*moicheia*) or an illicit love affair, but with a good will, openly, in lawful wedlock, abiding

---

[24] English text from Frank Williams' *The Panarion Of Epiphanius Of Salamis, Vols. 1* (Leiden: Brill, 1987, 1997) & 2 (Leiden: Brill, 1994).

by the faith, the commandments, good works, piety, fastings, good order, almsdeeds, zeal, the doing of good...'" (*Panarion, Heresy 59:6/ PG 41:1028*) "For example, not committing **fornication** (*porneuo*), not committing **adultery** (*moicheuo*), not being licentious, not having two spouses at once, not plundering, not being unjust, not getting drunk..." (*Panarion, Heresy 61:1/PG 41:1041*)

"Thus God's holy church does not accept **fornication** (*porneia*), **adultery** (*moicheia*), the denial of God, and those who defy the authority of God's ordinance and his apostles." (*Panarion, Heresy 61:4/PG 41:1044*)

John Chrysostom (c.347-407):

"There are set in us, like so many thorns, perjury, falsehood, hypocrisy, deceit, dishonesty, abusiveness, scoffing, buffoonery, indecency, scurrility; again under another head, covetousness, rapacity, injustice, calumny, insidiousness; again, wicked lust, uncleanness, lewdness, **fornication** (*porneia*), **adultery** (*moicheia*); again, envy, emulation, anger, wrath, rancor, revenge, blasphemy, and numberless others." (*Commentary On The Acts Of The Apostles, Homily 8 On Acts 3:1/ PG 60:72*)

"For this cause, even if a man do miracles, have celibacy to show, and fasting, and lying on the bare ground, and doth by this virtue advance even to the angels, yet shall he be most accursed of all, while he has this defect, and shall be a greater breaker of the Law than the **adulterer** (*moichos*), and the **fornicator** (*pornos*), and the robber, and the violator of sepulchers. (*Homilies On Romans, Homily 7 On Romans 3:9-18/ PG 60:448*)

"But what is filthiness of the flesh? **Adultery** (*moicheia*), **fornication** (*porneia*), lasciviousness of every kind." (*Commentary On 2nd Corinthians, Homily 13, Note On 2Corinthians 6:17/PG 61:494*)

"And speak not to me of those who have committed small sins, but suppose the case of one who is filled full of all wickedness, and let him practice everything which excludes him from the kingdom, and let us suppose that this man is not one of those who were unbelievers from the beginning, but formerly belonged to the believers, and such as were well pleasing to God, but afterwards has become a **fornicator** (*pornos*), **adulterer** (*moichos*), effeminate, a thief, a drunkard, a sodomite, a reviler, and everything else of this kind..." (*An Exhortation To Theodore After His Fall, Letter 1:4/ PG 47:281*)

"And if I see you persisting, I will forbid you for the future to set foot on this sacred threshold, and partake of the immortal mysteries; as we do fornicators (*porneuo*) and **adulterers** (*moicheuo*), and persons charged with murder. (*Homilies On Matthew, Homily 17 On Matthew 5:27-28/PG 57:264*)

"Let us "be merciful," not simply so, but "as our heavenly Father is." (Luke 6:36) He feeds even **adulterers** (*moichos*), and **fornicators** (*pornos*), and sorcerers, and what shall I say?" (*Homilies On Hebrews, Homily 11:10 On Hebrews 6:13-16/PG 63:96*)

"...just so these Greeks, as if they were really always children, (as some one also amongst themselves has said, the Greeks are always children,) fear those things that are no sins, such as filthiness of the body, the pollution of a funeral, a bed, or the keeping of days, and the like: whereas those which are really sins, unnatural lust, **adultery** (*moicheia*), **fornication** (*porneia*), of these they make no account at all. (*Homilies On Ephesians, Homily 12 On Ephesians 4:17/PG 62:92*)

"He would find persons who practice augury, who make use of charms, and omens and incantations, and who have committed **fornication** (*porneuo*), **adulterers** (*moicheuo*), drunkards, and revilers..." (*Homilies On Ephesians, Homily 6 On Ephesians 2:17-22/PG 62:48*)

"But these words he is now using concerning life and conduct. The Greeks are **fornicators** (*porneou*) and **adulterers** (*moicheuo*)." (*Homilies On Ephesians, Homily 12 On Ephesians 4:17/PG 62:91*)

"Ye see how he strips them of all excuse by speaking of "working uncleanness."...uncleanness is all **adultery** (*moicheia*), **fornication** (*porneia*), unnatural lust, envy, every kind of profligacy and lasciviousness." (*Homilies On Ephesians, Homily 13 On Ephesians 4:17-19/PG 62:94*)

"For the production of children, He implanted desire in thy mind, not for **fornication** (*porneia*), nor for **adultery** (*moicheia*)." (*Homilies On Philippians, Homily 10 On Philippians 3:1-3/PG 62:262*)

Pseudo-Hippolytus (4th-5th Cent.):
"**Fornications** (*porneia*), and **adulteries** (*moicheia*), and perjuries will fill the land; sorceries, and incantations, and divinations will follow after these with all force and zeal." (*A Discourse By The Most Blessed Hippolytus, Bishop And Martyr, On The End Of the World, And On Antichrist, And On The Second Coming Of Our Lord Jesus Christ, 7/PG 10:909*)

"And, on the whole, from among those who profess to be Christians will rise up then false prophets, false apostles, impostors, mischief-makers, evil-doers, liars against each other, **adulterers** (*moichos*), **fornicators** (*pornos*), robbers, grasping, perjured, mendacious, hating each other." (*A Discourse By The Most Blessed Hippolytus, Bishop And Martyr, On The End Of the World, And On Antichrist, And On The Second Coming Of Our Lord Jesus Christ, 7/PG 10:912*)

"But in his first steps he will be gentle, lovable, quiet, pious, pacific, hating injustice, detesting gifts, not allowing idolatry; loving, says he, the Scriptures, reverencing priests, honoring his elders, repudiating **fornication** (*porneia*), detesting **adultery** (*moicheia*), giving no heed to slanders, not admitting oaths, kind to strangers, kind to the poor, compassionate." (*A Discourse By The Most Blessed Hippolytus, Bishop And Martyr, On The End Of the World, And On Antichrist, And On The Second Coming Of Our Lord Jesus Christ, 23/PG 10:925*)

"The heaven shall be rolled together like a scroll: the whole earth shall be burnt up by reason of the deeds done in it, which men did corruptly, in **fornications** (*porneia*), in **adulteries** (*moicheia*), and in lies and uncleanness, and in idolatries, and in murders, and in battles." (*A Discourse By The Most Blessed Hippolytus, Bishop And Martyr, On The End Of the World, And On Antichrist, And On The Second Coming Of Our Lord Jesus Christ, 37/PG 10:940*)

"I ordained your feet to walk in the preparation of the Gospel of peace, both in the churches and the houses of my saints; and ye taught them to run to **adulteries** (*moicheia*), and **fornications** (*porneia*), and theaters, and dancings, and elevations." (*A Discourse By The Most Blessed Hippolytus, Bishop And Martyr, On The End Of the World, And On Antichrist, And On The Second Coming Of Our Lord Jesus Christ, 46/PG 10:948*)

Clementine Homilies (4th-5th Cent.):

"For whenever the soul is sown by others, then it is forsaken by the Spirit, as guilty of **fornication** (*porneuo*) or **adultery** (*moicheuo*); and so the living body, the life-giving Spirit being withdrawn, is dissolved into dust, and the rightful punishment of sin is suffered at the time of the judgment by the soul, after the dissolution of the body..." (*Homily 3:28/PG 2:129*)

Theodoret (c.393-c.457):

"Then for divine words he uttered shameless wickedness, for awful doctrines wanton lewdness, for piety impiety, for continence **fornication** (*porneia*), **adultery** (*moicheia*), foul lust, theft; teaching that gluttony and drunkenness as well as all the rest were good for man's life." (*Church History, 4:19/PG 82:1169*)

It should be clear after reading the above quotes that Greek writers generally understood the *porneia* family of words to refer to something *different than* and *distinct from* adultery. They would not have used the two word families in the above manner if they had understood them to mean the same thing.

Interestingly, the evidence in favor of *porneia* referring to pre-marital sex is so strong that even some people who believe in the Adultery View will acknowledge that this is the normal and general usage of it. John Conington, in discussing the Fornication View, notes that it "has the advantage of giving a sense to *porneia* which no one can dispute"[25] and Henry Tebbs writes that "*Porneia*...is frequently employed to express simple fornication between unmarried persons..."[26] Likewise, R. H. Charles acknowledges that the debate over the Adultery View revolves around "*porneia*, which usually means 'fornication'..."[27] If even men who believe in the Adultery View are acknowledging that no one can dispute that *porneia* usually means pre-marital sex why are we holding on so strongly to the Adultery View? Are we allowing emotion to guide our theology rather than the plain reading of the Scripture?

The King James Translation
Committee And Numerous Other Translators
Whose Translations Favored The Fornication View

Another factor that played a part in me changing my mind on the Adultery View is that, as noted above, the **Fornication View** is reflected in the King James Version's translation of Matthew 19:9a which they translated as:

---

[25] *On Dollinger's Interpretation About Christ's Precept About Divorce* in *Contemporary Review, Vol. 11: May-August, 1869* (London: Strahan & Co. Publishers, 1869), p.4.
[26] *Essay On The Scripture Doctrines Of Adultery And Divorce* (London: F.C. & J. Rivington, 1822), p.86.
[27] *The Teaching Of The New Testament On Divorce* (London: William & Norgate, 1921), p.23.

And I say unto you, Whosoever shall put away his wife, except it be for <u>fornication</u>, and shall marry another, committeth adultery:

It has been alleged that in 1611, the year that the King James Version was published, that the word "fornication" was understood by English speakers to include the idea of adultery. However, *this allegation is just simply not true* and it is easy to demonstrate why. In 1604, six years before the King James Version was completed, Robert Cawdrey published one of the first English language dictionaries in London. In it he gave the common English understanding of the word "fornication" and his entire definition was as follows:

fornication, vncleannes betweene single persones.[28]

And it wasn't just Cawdrey's dictionary that defined it this way. Dictionaries before, at the time of and well after the time of the King James Version defined "fornication" as sexual behavior by *single people*.

Edmund Coote's
***The English Schoole-Maister* (1596):** *fornication*: vncleannes betweene single persons.[29]

Thomas Blount's
***Gloffographia Anglicana* (1656):** *Fornication*: Whoredom, Leachery, spoken of single persons, if either party be married then tis *Adultery*.[30]

R. Brown's
***The English Expofitor Improv'd* (1719):** *fornication*. Whoredom committed between single Persons, whereas if either, or both Parties so

---

[28] *A Table Alphabeticall, Conteyning and Teaching the True Writing, and Vnderstanding of Hard Vsuall English Wordes, Borrowed from the Hebrew, Greeke, Latine, or French. &c. With the Interpretation Thereof by Plaine English Words, Gathered for the Benefit & Helpe of Ladies, Gentlewomen, or Any Other Vnskilfull Persons* (London: Printed by I. R. for Edmund Weauer, 1604).
[29] *The English Schoole-Maister* (London: Printed by the Widow Orwin, for Ralph Iackson and Robert Dexter, 1596).
[30] *Gloffographia Anglicana* Reprint of First Edition, (Hildesheim: G. Olms, 1972).

offending be married, it is called Adultery, and is punishable with Death by the Common Law.[31]

John Kersey's
The New World Of Words **(1720):** *Fornication,* the Act of uncleanness between single Persons, so call'd because usually committed in Stews, under Vaults or Arches, in *Latin, Fornices.*[32]

The word "fornication" was not understood by 17th century English speakers to carry with it the idea of adultery. Instead it was understood the way that modern readers understand the term—*a reference to pre-marital sexual relations.* And this is evident not only from dictionaries made around the time of the King James Version but from English literature dating back hundreds of years prior to 1611.

In 1303 Robert Manning wrote a devotional book entitled *Handlyng Synne* (Handling Sin) in which he encouraged people to turn from their sins. In it he clearly showed that the term fornication referred to premarital sex and was something *different than* adultery.

Middle English	Modern English
Þe first ys '**fornycacyon**,'	The first is '**fornication**,'
whan two vnweddyd haue mysdon,	when two unmarried have misdone,
As sengle knaue and sengle tarne,	As single boy and single girl,
whan þey synne to-gedyr ȝerne;	When they sin together eagerly;
Þe leste hyt ys of allë seuene,	The least it is of all seven[34],

---

[31] *The English Expofitor Improv'd: Being A Complete Dictionary, Teaching The Interpretation Of The Moft Difficult Words, Which Are Commonly Made Ufe Of In Our Englifh Tongue* (London: Printed for W. Churchill at the Black-Swan in Paternoster-Row, 1719).

[32] *The New World Of Words: or, Universal English Dictionary* (London: Printed for J. Philips, 1720).

[33] Frederick James Furnivall, *Robert of Brunne's "Handlyng Synne," A.D. 1303: With Those Parts Of The Anglo-French Treatise On Which It Was Founded, William of Wadington's "Manuel Des Pechiez,"*, Vol. 2 (London: Kegal Paul, Trench, Trübner & Co., Ltd., 1903), p. 235.

ȝyt hyt forbarreþ þe blys of heuene.	Yet it causes one to lose the bliss of heaven.
Þe touþer ys **awoutry,**	The other is **adultery,**
Whan weddyd and weddyd to-gedyr lye	When a married person and a married person together have intercourse
As weddyd man takeþ anoþers wife,	As a married man takes the wife of another,
Þat ys þe morë sinful lyfe.	That is the more sinful life.
ȝyf weddyd man, sengle woman takeþ,	If a married man, a single woman takes,
Forsoþe spousebrechë þere he makyþ.	Indeed a breach of the marriage vow he here makes.
ȝyf weddyd wife take sengle man,	If a married woman takes a single man,
Alle spousebreche tel y hyt þan;	All breach of the marriage vow tell it to that man;
For þey haue broke with-outë fayle	For they have broken without fail
Þe chastë bondë of spousayle.	The chaste bond of marriage.
-*Handlyng Synne*, lines 7351-7366[33]	-*Handling Sin*, lines 7351-7366

John de Thoresby (d. 1373) was the Archbishop of Canterbury and in 1357 he published an English version of *The Lay Folk's Catechism* (a manual for new converts to Christianity) and commanded all of the English clergy to read it diligently unto their parishioners.[35] This meant that every English preacher was required by the highest ranking English bishop to read this book to their entire congregation. Notice how Thoresby's catechism indicated that "fornication" was not the same thing as "adultery".

Middle English	Modern English

---

[34] That is, of the seven-fold nature of the sin of *lechery* (lust) which this passage is discussing.

[35] Thomas Frederick Simmons & Henry Edward Nolloth, eds., *The Lay Folks' Catechism; or, The English And Latin Versions Of Archbishop Thoresby's Instruction For The People* (London: Kegal Paul, Trench, Trübner & Co., Ltd., 1901). p. xxv.

The seuent deadly syn is lecheri,	The seventh deadly sin is lechery,
That is a foule liking or lust of the flesch;	This is a foul desire or lust of the flesh;
And of this syn comes many sere spices.	And from this sin comes many different kinds [of sins].
Ane is **fornication**, a fleshly syn	One is **fornication**, a fleshly sin
Betwix ane aynlepi man, and ane aynlepi woman,	Between one unmarried man and one unmarried woman,
That forthi that it is ogaynes the lawe	Because it is against the law
And the leue, and the lare that hali kirk haldes,	And the permission, and the tradition that holy church observes,
It is deadly syn to tham that dos it.	It is deadly sin to them that do it.
An other is **auoutry**, that is spousebrek,	Another is **adultery**, that is a breach of the marriage vow,
Whether it be bodily or it be gastely,	Whether it is done bodily or with an incubus/succubus,
That greuouser and gretter is than the other.	It (adultery) is more grievous and greater [a sin] than the other [sin of fornication].
-*The Lay Folk's Catechism*, lines 542-553[36]	-*The Lay Folk's Catechism*, lines 542-553

By having the highest ranking bishop of England require that the above distinction between fornication and adultery be taught and read to all congregations in the land the common understanding of fornication amongst English speakers would have been that it was something *different* than adultery.

Around the same time John Wycliffe (c.1324-1384) prepared his own version of *The Lay Folk's Catechism* and he again made a clear distinction between "fornication" not being the same thing as "adultery".

---

[36] Thomas Frederick Simmons & Henry Edward Nolloth, eds., *The Lay Folks' Catechism; or, The English And Latin Versions Of Archbishop Thoresby's Instruction For The People* (London: Kegal Paul, Trench, Trübner & Co., Ltd., 1901). p.94-96.

Middle English	Modern English
The vij. dedly synne and þe laste ys leccherye	The seventh and last deadly sin is lechery
Þat is stynkynge lykyng or lust of þe flesche.	It is a foul desiring or lust of the flesh.
and of þis syn comyþ many sere spicys.	And of this sin comes many different kinds [of sins].
On is **fornicacioun** of fleschly synne	One is **fornication** of fleshly sin
be-twene a sengyl man and a sengyl womman	between a single man and a single woman
and for þat is gayn þe law.	And for that is against the law
and leue and þe lore / þat holy chirche holdis.	and the permission and the tradition that the holy church holds.
yt is dedly synne to hem þat doþ yt.	It is a deadly sin to him that does it.
Anoþer is **avowtri**. Þat ys spowse-brekynge	Another is **adultery**. That is a breaking of the marriage vow
wheþer it be bodyly or gostly.	Whether it is done bodily or with an incubus/succubus spirit.
wel greuouser yt is and gretter þan þe oþer.	Well graver it is and greater [a sin] than the other [sin of fornication].
-*The Lay Folk's Catechism*, lines 1392-1402[37]	-*The Lay Folk's Catechism*, lines 1392-1402

If the King James Translation Committee did not want the average English reader to understand the exception clause to refer to sexual behavior *before* marriage then it is very unclear as to why they translated it in such a way that the English speaking world would have understood it to mean so. The KJV translators purposefully chose a word which they knew the common man would understand to mean *pre-nuptial sin*.

---

[37] Thomas Frederick Simmons & Henry Edward Nolloth, eds., *The Lay Folks' Catechism; or, The English And Latin Versions Of Archbishop Thoresby's Instruction For The People* (London: Kegal Paul, Trench, Trübner & Co., Ltd., 1901). p.95-97.

If the King James Translation Committee had been meeting in our day and wanted to translate this passage with the same meaning that a 1611 reader would have understood it to have they would be forced to translate it in the following way:

And I say unto you, Whosoever shall put away his wife, except it be for <u>pre-marital sex</u>, and shall marry another, committeth adultery:

After reading above how that the word family of *porneia* was used in Greek literature from the 4th century BC until the 5th century AD one can understand why the King James Committee translated this passage in the way that they did. And it will also help to explain why so many English translations have translated the exception clause as "fornication" and not "adultery".

1. **The Great Bible:** "except it be for fornicacion"
2. **Bishop's Bible:** "except it be for fornication"
3. **Matthew Bible:** "except it be for fornication"
4. **Tyndale New Testament:** "except it be for fornicacion"
5. **King James Version 1611:** "except it be for fornication"
6. **American Standard Version:** "except for fornication"
7. **English Revised Version:** "except for fornication"
8. **Literal Translation Of The Bible:** "if not for fornication"
9. **Primitive New Testament:** "cause of fornication"
10. **American Baptist Publication Society Version:** "except for fornication"
11. **King James 1769 Oxford Revision:** "except it be for fornication"
12. **American Bible Union Version:** "except for fornication"
13. **New Testament In The Common Version:** "except it be for fornication"
14. **Granville Penn New Testament:** "except on account of fornication"
15. **J.T. Conquest Bible:** "except it be for fornication"
16. **Herman Heinfetter New Testament:** "saving for a cause of fornication"
17. **George R. Noyes New Testament:** "except for fornication"
18. **Frank Schell Ballentine Version:** "except for fornication"

19. **Ferrar Fenton Bible:** "unless for fornication"
20. **A. S. Worrell New Testament:** "except for fornication"
21. **Samuel Lloyd New Testament:** "unless it be for fornication"
22. **Samuel Sharpe New Testament:** "save for fornication"
23. **Spencer Cone & William Wyckoff New Testament:** "except for fornication"
24. **Rotherham New Testament Version:** "not on the ground of fornication"
25. **James Moffatt New Testament:** "except for fornication"
26. **Moulton's Modern Reader's Bible:** "except for fornication"
27. **Bible In Modern English:** "except for fornication"
28. **Dillard New Testament:** "except it be for fornication"
29. **Julia Smith Bible:** "except for fornication"
30. **Palfrey's New Testament:** "except it be for fornication"
31. **Scrivener's Cambridge Paragraph Bible:** "except it be for fornication"
32. **George Berry Interlinear Literal Translation:** "if not for fornication"
33. **Samuel Davidson New Testament:** "except for fornication"
34. **John Darby New Testament:** "not for fornication"
35. **Henry Alford New Testament:** "except for fornication"
36. **T. J. Hussey New Testament:** "except it be for fornication"
37. **W. B. Godbey New Testament:** "not for fornication"
38. **Edward Clarke New Testament:** "except it be for fornication"
39. **The Bible Designed To Be Read As Living Literature:** "except it be for fornication"
40. **Charles C. Torrey's Four Gospels Translation:** "except on the ground of fornication"
41. **Robert Ainslie New Testament:** "except for fornication"
42. **H. Hammond New Testament Paraphrase:** "for any lesser cause than that of fornication"
43. **Henry Highton New Testament:** "except it be for fornication"
44. **Green's Literal Version:** "if not for fornication"
45. **American King James Version:** "except it be for fornication"
46. **Updated King James Version:** "except it be for fornication"
47. **Modern King James Version (Green):** "except for fornication"
48. **E. V. Rieu Four Gospels Translation:** "except it be for fornication"

49. **King James 2000 Version:** "except it be for fornication"
50. **New Authorized Version of the Bible (AV7):** "except it be for fornication"
51. **21ˢᵗ Century King James Version:** "except it be for fornication"
52. **The Byzantine Majority New Testament:** "except it be for fornication"
53. **English Jubilee 2000 Bible:** "except [it be] for fornication"
54. **A Conservative Version:** "not for fornication"
55. **King James Clarified New Testament:** "unless it be for fornication"
56. **King James Version (Corrected Edition):** "except it be for fornication"
57. **Yes Word (Revised Tyndale):** "except it be for fornication"
58. **Third Millennium Bible:** "except it be for fornication"
59. **King James Version Easy Reading:** "except it be for fornication"
60. **Modern Literal Version:** "not for fornication"

Even some of the newer translations which have chosen to translate this passage in such a way as to convey the idea of adultery (despite the Greek literary evidence discouraging this) sometimes include footnotes indicating that the word could also be translated or literally means "fornication". These include some editions of the New American Standard Version and the New King James Version. Their decision to do so implies that the translators were not comfortable in translating *porneia* in such a way as to make the exception clause mean "except for adultery".

The Apparent Contradiction Between Matthew 19:9a And Luke 16:18 Which Arises Under The Adultery View

One of the strongest reasons for me rejecting the Adultery View in favor of the Fornication View is the fact that if one accepts the Adultery View then it actually causes two statements of Jesus regarding divorce and remarriage to contradict each other.

The modern interpretation of the Adultery View goes something like this:

As soon one partner in the marriage commits adultery the other innocent spouse is free to divorce and remarry. If a divorce happens without adultery having been committed, say for example a husband waits until after he has divorced his wife and then has sexual relations with another woman, then as soon as the adultery has actually occurred the Matthean exception clause goes into affect and the innocent wife is free to remarry.

The problem with this interpretation is that in Luke 16:18 Jesus describes just such a situation where a husband divorces his wife and *then* has sexual relations with another woman yet Jesus seems to say that the innocent wife in this event *is not allowed to remarry*.

Whoever puts away his wife, and marries another, commits adultery and whoever marries her that is put away from her husband commits adultery. Lk 16:18

I read this passage for years and never really noticed that it was clearly contradicting the Adultery View. In the above passage Jesus says that there was a husband who divorced his wife and married another person. The Lord is clear in this scenario that the husband "commits adultery" in his sexual relations with his new wife. However, notice what Jesus says to the *innocent party* in this situation. He says of the innocent woman whose husband has left and <u>committed adultery</u> that "whoever marries her...*commits adultery*" also. This verse is really one of the strongest pieces of evidence against the Adultery View because it plainly and clearly shows that the innocent spouse, whose husband has "committed adultery", is *not free* to remarry and that if she does she herself commits the sin of adultery. I am not aware of any modern day Adultery View writers who have even attempted to explain this discrepancy. I honestly believe that the main reason that no Adultery View writer has even attempted to address this issue is because Luke 16:18 is so easy to overlook. I read this passage for years while teaching the Adultery View and never once noticed that it was saying that a woman whose husband had committed adultery was not allowed to remarry.

The Fornication View Matches An Actual Reference

28

To Concealed Pre-nuptial Sin In The Law Of Moses

Another factor that influenced me to reject the Adultery View in favor of the Fornication View was that the exception clause appeared to be referring to an actual law in the Old Testament which dealt with concealed pre-nuptial sin. When Jesus gave the exception clause in Matthew 19 he indicated that:

Whoever shall put away his wife, except it be for <u>fornication</u> (*porneia*)**, and shall marry another, commits adultery... Mt 19:9a**

The Fornication View interprets this passage to be referring to a woman who has secretly committed pre-nuptial sin, kept this from her husband to be, and then has her sin discovered *after* the wedding. Remember that Matthew was written in Greek and that its author relied upon the Greek translation of the Hebrew Old Testament known as the Septuagint and in the Law of Moses (Dt 22:13-21) there is a law regarding a woman who *secretly commits pre-nuptial sin, keeps it from her husband to be, and then has her sin discovered after the wedding*. In the Septuagint's translation of this passage the action of the woman's *pre-nuptial sin* is translated using the *porneia* family of words:

"And if any one should take a wife, and dwell with her, and hate her, and attach to her reproachful words, and bring against her an evil name, and say, I took this woman, and when I came to her **I found not her tokens of virginity**: then the father and the mother of the damsel shall take and bring out the damsel's tokens of virginity to the elders of the city to the gate...But if this report be true, and the tokens of virginity be not found for the damsel; then shall they bring out the damsel to the doors of her father's house, and shall stone her with stones, and she shall die; because she has wrought folly among the children of Israel, to defile the house of her father by **whoring** (*ek-porneuo*): so thou shalt remove the evil one from among you." (Dt 22:13-21Brenton)

So, the very Greek family of words that Jesus uses in the exception clause can be traced directly back to a reference in the Law of Moses referring to *concealed, pre-nuptial sin*. It seems realistic to believe that

29

Greek speaking Jews who were familiar with the Septuagint would have been more likely to be reminded of this passage when they read Jesus' exception clause for *porneia* than they would have been of "Thou shalt not commit adultery (*moicheuo*)". This is a strong evidence for accepting the Fornication View in favor of the Adultery View.

The Theological Underpinnings
Supporting The Fornication View

Another factor that strongly influenced my decision to adopt the Fornication View over the Adultery View was that there was a clear theological argument in favor of the Fornication View. One might rightfully ask *is there any reason why concealed pre-marital sex would be considered by God as justification for a man to put away his wife*. Theologically there is a valid reason and it comes from understanding the *covenantal* nature of marriage.

The Bible indicates that when two people enter into a marriage they are actually entering into a *covenant* with each other:

> **Yet you say, 'Why?' Because the LORD has been witness between you and the wife of your youth, against whom you have dealt treacherously: yet she is your companion, and the wife of your <u>covenant</u>. Mal 2:14**

A covenant, generally speaking, is defined as an agreement entered into by two parties with certain requirements expected of either side. Linguistically, the Hebrew word for covenant (*beriyth*) carries with it the idea of "cutting":

> **Gesenius' *Hebrew And Chaldee Lexicon To The Old Testament Scriptures*:** "*beriyth* f.— (1) *a covenant,* so called from the idea of <u>cutting</u> (see the root No. 1), since it was the custom in making solemn covenants to pass between the divided parts of [animal] victims…"[38]

---

[38] Wilhelm Gesenius & Samuel Prideaux Tregelles, Tr. (New York: J. Wiley & Sons, 1893), p.141.

Pike's *A Compendious Hebrew Lexicon:* "*beriyth* –to <u>cut</u> *off*...to make a covenant; alluding to the antient manner of doing it as described, Gen. xv.10, 18. Jer. xxxiv. 18, 19."[39]

Davies' *Student's Hebrew Lexicon:* "*beriyth* –f. prop. <u>*cutting*</u> *up* (of beasts in sacrifice, see *barah*); hence fig. *contract* or *covenant* Gen. 21, 27; perh. the custom was for the covenanting parties to pass between the parts of the <u>cut</u> up victim (Gen. 15, 10)."[40]

When people entered into a covenant with God in the Bible there was noticeably always a "cutting" or "separating" of a living creature that resulted in its blood being shed. This is evident in the covenants that God made between Himself and Noah, Abraham, Abraham's descendants, Moses, and the Christians through Jesus Christ.

Noahic Covenant

In Genesis 8:20-9:17 Noah is recorded as sacrificing animals (which would have involved cutting them and allowing their blood to spill out) after which God enters into a covenant with him.	"And Noah built an altar unto the LORD; and took of every clean beast, and of every clean bird, and <u>offered burnt offerings</u> on the altar. And the LORD smelled a sweet savor; and the LORD said in his heart, I will not again curse the ground any more for man's sake...And God spoke unto Noah, and to his sons with him, saying, 'And I, behold, <u>I establish my covenant with you</u>, and with your seed after you...'"

Abrahamic Covenant

In Genesis 15:7-21 when God promises Abraham that He will give unto his descendants the land	"And he said unto him, 'I am the LORD that brought you out of Ur of the Chaldees, to give you this land

---

[39] Samuel Pike, *Second Cambridge Edition,* (Cambridge: Printed by Hilliard & Metcalf, for the University, 1811), p.69.
[40] Benjamin Davies, (London: Asher & Co., 1872), p.104-105.

extending from the Nile to the Euphrates Rivers Abraham takes a young cow, a goat and a ram and cuts them in half (thus spilling their blood) after which God enters into a covenant with him to give his posterity the land.	to inherit it.' And he said, 'LORD God, whereby shall I know that I shall inherit it?' And he said unto him, 'Take me an heifer of three years old, and a she goat of three years old, and a ram of three years old, and a turtledove, and a young pigeon.' And he took unto him all these, and <u>divided</u> (i.e. cut) them down the middle, and laid each piece one against another: but the birds divided he not...And it came to pass, that, when the sun went down, and it was dark, behold there was a smoking furnace, and a burning lamp that passed between those pieces. In the same day the LORD <u>made a covenant</u> with Abram..."

Covenant Of Circumcision

In Genesis 17:7-14 God instructs Abraham that in order for his descendants to continue in the covenant relationship with him that every male must has his foreskin cut off (thus shedding blood). Any individuals who did not experience this cutting and spilling of blood would not be in the covenant relationship with God.	"And I will establish my <u>covenant</u> between me and you and your seed after you in their generations for an everlasting <u>covenant</u>...This is my <u>covenant,</u> which ye shall keep, between me and you and your seed after you; Every man child among you shall be <u>circumcised</u>. And ye shall <u>circumcise</u> the flesh of your foreskin; and it shall be <u>a token of the covenant</u> between me and you...And the uncircumcised man child whose flesh of his foreskin is not circumcised, that soul shall be cut off from his people; he hath broken my <u>covenant</u>."

Mosaic Covenant	
In Exodus 20:1-23:33 God instructs Moses to tell the Israelites how He expects them to behave if they are to be in a covenant relationship with Him. After telling the people what God requires of them Moses then has animals sacrificed (which involved cutting and the subsequent shedding of their blood). He then read to the Israelites what God expected of them and they agreed to obey it, thus entering into a covenant with Him.	"And Moses wrote all the words of the LORD, and rose up early in the morning, and built an altar under the hill, and twelve pillars, according to the twelve tribes of Israel. And he sent young men of the children of Israel, which offered <u>burnt offerings</u>, and <u>sacrificed peace offerings of oxen</u> unto the LORD. And Moses took half of the <u>blood</u>, and put it in basins; and half of the <u>blood</u> he sprinkled on the altar. And he took the book of the <u>covenant</u>, and read in the audience of the people: and they said, 'All that the LORD has said we will do, and be obedient.' And Moses took the <u>blood</u>, and sprinkled it on the people, and said, 'Behold the <u>blood</u> of the <u>covenant</u>, which the LORD has made with you concerning all these words.'" (Ex 24:4-8)
The New Covenant	
In Matthew 26:27-28 as Jesus was having the last supper with His disciples He explained to them that His blood was going to be shed so that God might enter into a New Covenant with humanity. The next day He experienced his flesh being cut through being whipped, nailed to a cross and pierced with a spear which resulted in the spilling of His blood.	"And he took the cup, and gave thanks, and gave it to them, saying, 'Drink ye all of it; For this is my blood of the new <u>covenant</u>, which is <u>shed</u> for many for the remission of sins."

In each of these covenants there is a noticeable cutting, separating and shedding of blood and when two people enter into a covenant marriage there is also, generally speaking, a cutting, separating and shedding of blood. This is because when a virgin woman enters into a marriage and the husband inserts his penis into her vagina for the first time he will unavoidably end up separating and *rupturing* the hymen, a fold of mucous membrane that surrounds or partially covers the external vaginal opening, resulting in *cutting* and *bleeding*. This is why there is often blood on the sheets the morning after the wedding night. This "cutting", "separating" and subsequent "shedding of blood" is the act of entering into covenant with one another. God designed the first sex act to operate in such a way as to meet the standards of entering into a covenant.

This is why a *concealed, pre-marital sexual experience* would allow a man to put away his wife and marry another and explains the theological reasoning behind Matthew's "exception clause". If a woman was not a virgin and concealed this from her husband it gave the man a right to call off his marriage according to Jesus' in Matthew 19:9a because *the one act which made a marriage a marriage (i.e. the creation of a covenant) could not be recreated if a woman had already ruptured her hymen in a previous sexual experience.* Jesus' exception clause does not contradict his other very strict prohibitions against divorce and remarriage[41] because in a case where a woman has already ruptured her hymen with another man and then concealed this from her husband a covenant marriage actually never took place. This is why a man is justified in "putting away" his wife in the case of fornication, simply because in God's eyes she had never really became his wife because she had done something to keep herself from entering into covenant with her husband to be.

The understanding that a woman needed to marry the person who ruptured her hymen is clearly presented in the Old Testament. If two unmarried people had intercourse the man was required to approach the girl's father and ask for marriage:

If a man finds a young woman that is a virgin, who is not betrothed, and lays hold of her, and lies with her, and they are found out; then the man that laid with her shall give unto the

---

[41] Mk 10:11-12, Lk 16:18

young woman's father fifty shekels of silver, and she shall be his wife; because he has humbled her, he may not put her away all his days. Dt 22:28-29

And if a man entices a virgin that is not betrothed, and lies with her, he shall surely pay the dowry price for her to be his wife. If her father utterly refuses to give her unto him, he shall pay money according to the dowry price of virgins. Ex 22:16-17

Unless the father had an objection the two people had *no choice* but to marry. This was because the young woman's decision to engage in pre-marital sex had, in some way, affected her ability to enter into a covenant marriage with another man. Generally, the hymen only ruptures and sheds blood once and in the case of pre-marital sex once it is ruptured it is ruptured.[42]

Medical Literature And The Rupturing Of The Hymen

In modern times there has been a concerted effort on the part of many feminists to downplay the rupturing of the hymen and, therefore, we need to see what medical literature says about the tearing of the hymen at the first intercourse.

---

[42] Of course, all of this does not mean that women who have committed sexual sin can never rightfully marry anyone else aside from their first sexual partner. That would be the ideal but in many cases women have had sexual experiences only to marry other men. The "Exception Clause" of Matthew 19:9a is dealing with a situation where the wife has *secretly* engaged in fornication and withheld this information from her husband, only to have him discover it *after* the wedding. If a woman has engaged in fornication with one man and then, for whatever reason, desires to marry a different man she must confess all of her sexual transgressions to her fiancé *before* the wedding so that her husband-to-be can make his decision to marry her knowing all of her past. If a husband knows of his wife-to-be's sexual fornication but decides to marry her anyway he cannot in any way use the exception clause because it only deals with the experience of a man discovering the truth of his wife's lack of virginity *after* the marriage.

Textbook Of Forensic Medicine And Toxicology: "It is *usually ruptured at the time of the first sexual intercourse.*"[43]

Homeopathy In Obstetrics And Paediatrics: "The hymen is the delicate membranous structure, which covers the greater portion of the orifice of the vagina,—and which *is usually ruptured at the first successful attempt at sexual intercourse.*"[44]

Common Diseases Of Women: "*During the first intercourse the hymen gets ruptured,* resulting in mild pain, soreness and bleeding."[45]

Clinical Obstetrics: "Usually the hymen is circular or somewhat crescentic and *is usually ruptured at the first coitus.* An intact hymen is considered a sign of virginity."[46]

A Comprehensive Textbook of Midwifery: "The hymen is *usually ruptured at the consummation* of marriage."[47]

Sexuality Now, Embracing Diversity: "If the hymen is intact, it will *usually rupture easily and tear at several points during the first intercourse,* often accompanied by a small amount of blood."[48]

Sex for Dummies: "If your hymen is already broken, then having sex for the first time probably won't cause you any pain or bleeding. If your hymen is not broken, then you may feel some pain, *and you will bleed a little.*"[49]

Sperm Competition In Humans: Classic And Contemporary Readings: "Although the structure may be ruptured by activities other than sexual intercourse, *usually the first coitus breaks the hymen,* causing female pain and bleeding."[50]

---

[43] Nageshkumar G. Rao, (New Delhi: Jaypee Brothers Medical Publishers, 2006), p.283.

[44] Henry N. Guernsey, (New Delhi: B. Jain Publishers, Ltd., 2005), p.32.

[45] Renu Gupta, (New Delhi: Diamond Pocket Books, 2006), p.17.

[46] Sarala Gopalan & Vanita Jain, *Tenth Edition,* (Chennai: Orient Longman Pvt. Ltd., 2006), p.10.

[47] Annama Jacob, (New Delhi: Jaypee Brothers Medical Publishers, 2008), p.53.

[48] Janell L. Carroll, (Belmont, CA: Wadsworth, 2010), p.120.

[49] Ruth K. Westheimer & Pierre A. Lehu, *Third Edition,* (Hoboken, NJ: Wiley Publishing, 2007), p.137.

[50] Todd K. Shackelford & Nicholas Pound, eds., Robert L. Smith, *Human Sperm Competition* (New York, NY: Springer Science Business Media, 2006), p.102.

Encyclopedia of Family Health: "In most cases, the thin membrane will be in place and will break the first time the woman has intercourse."[51]

Women's Sexual Health: "It is stretched during sexual intercourse and *the first coitus usually causes slight bleeding.*"[52]

Encyclopaedia of AIDS and Sexual Behavior: "Defloration: the rupture of the hymen, which *usually occurs during the first experience of intercourse.*"[53]

Sexual Reproductive Health of Young People: "If the hymen is present, it will *usually rupture and tear at several points during the first intercourse,* this is accompanied by slight bleeding and discomfort."[54]

So the medical literature seems to be in agreement that the usual experience is that the hymen *will rupture* upon the first act of intercourse. However, some women who did marry as virgins report not experiencing a rupturing of their hymens. There was not pain, nor was there blood present after the intercourse. Two common reasons for this are that 1.) The experience of pain is often over exaggerated; and 2.) When the hymen ruptures it usually only produces a little bit of blood.

1.) The experience of pain is often over exaggerated. The pain associated with the rupturing of the hymen is not an overwhelming pain and it takes place at a very emotional and exciting time for the woman. Many women are surely so preoccupied with the newness of their first sexual experience that they do not pay as much attention to pain as they normally would. Contrary to popular belief it is not an experience of excruciating pain.

2.) When the hymen ruptures it usually only produces a little bit of blood. Medical literature also agrees that when the hymen does rupture upon first intercourse the bleeding is normally *very minimal*:

David Humphreys Storer, M.D.: "In most cases the hymen is ruptured with but little pain and *trifling* hemorrhage."[55]

---

[51] David B. Jacoby & R. M. Youngson, eds., (Tarrytown, NY: Marshall Cavendish, 2005), p.2368.

[52] Gilly Andrews, *Third Edition*, (Edinburgh: Elsevier, Ltd., 2005), p.516.

[53] B. K. Sinha, ed. (New Delhi: Anmol Publications Pvt. Ltd., 1999), p.175.

[54] M. K. C. Nair, (New Delhi: Jaypee Brothers Medical Publishers, 2006), p.15.

A. E. Giles, M.D., M.R.C.P.: "Bleeding from a tear of the hymen itself is always *inconsiderable*…"[56]

Elizabeth G. Stewart, M.D.: "Despite the folkloric image of enthusiastic villagers waving a stained bedsheet after a wedding night to prove the bride had been successfully deflowered, the hymen has few blood vessels, so bleeding is *minimal*."[57]

John Cooke Hirst, M.D.: "The bleeding from rupture of the hymen at coitus is normally *negligible*…"[58]

Thomas Watts Eden, M.D.: "The *slight* bleeding which usually attends a first coitus is due to laceration of the hymen…"[59]

Henry N. Guernsey, M.D.: "The rupture of this structure ordinarily occasions a *slight* flow of blood…"[60]

Janell L. Carroll, Ph.D., C.S.E.: "If the hymen is intact, it will usually rupture easily…often accompanied by a *small amount* of blood."[61]

Ruth K. Westheimer, Ed.D.: "If your hymen is not broken, then you may feel some pain, and you will bleed a *little*."[62]

Gilly Andrews, R.G.N., E.N.B & Jill Steele, R.N., R.H.V.: "…the first coitus usually causes *slight* bleeding."[63]

M. K. C. Nair, M.D., Ph.D., M.Sc.: "If the hymen is present, it will usually rupture…this is accompanied by *slight* bleeding and discomfort."[64]

---

[55] *Reports Of Medical Societies* in *The Boston Medical And Surgical Journal, January 12, 1871, Vol. 8, No.2* republished in *The Boston Medical And Surgical Journal, Vol. 84,* (Boston: David Clapp & Son, 1871), p.24.

[56] Entry for *Vulva, Disease Of The* in *Encyclopedia Medica, Vol. 13,* (New York, NY: Longmans, Green & Co., 1903), p.423.

[57] *The V Book: A Doctor's Guide To Complete Vulvovaginal Health,* (New York, NY: Random House, Inc., 2002), Ch.4, p.67.

[58] *A Manual Of Gynecology,* (Philadelphia, PA: W.B. Saunders Co., 1918), p.48.

[59] *Gynecology For Students And Practitioners,* (New York, NY: The Macmillan Co., 1920), p.133.

[60] *Homeopathy In Obstetrics And Paediatrics,* (New Delhi: B. Jain Publishers, Ltd., 2005), p.32.

[61] *Sexuality Now: Embracing Diversity,* (Belmont, CA: Wadsworth, 2010), p.120.

[62] *Sex For Dummies, Third Edition,* (Hoboken, NJ: Wiley Publishing, 2007), p.137.

[63] *Women's Sexual Health, Third Edition,* (Edinburgh: Elsevier, Ltd., 2005), p.516.

[64] *Sexual Reproductive Health Of Young People,* (New Delhi: Jaypee Brothers Medical Publishers, 2006), p.15.

Many people probably did bleed in their first sexual experience but just didn't realize it because the blood loss can be of such a *small nature*. It is entirely possible that many times the hymen is ruptured but the blood loss is so small that the parties involved do not even notice. How many couples really make it a point to do a thorough investigation after their first intercourse to look for the blood?

The Fornication View Is Contained In Natural Law

The New Testament describes how that God has placed his natural moral law upon the hearts of all men and women. In the book of Romans Paul explains this phenomena by pointing out that *"when the Gentiles, which have not the law, do by nature the things contained in the law, these, having not the law, are a law unto themselves, who show the work of the law written in their hearts…* (Rom 2:14-15)." This explains why all cultures view things like murder, stealing and disobeying one's parents as wrong, regardless of whether they have ever had Christianity preached there or not. Further evidence for the **Fornication View** being the correct interpretation of Matthew 19:9a is its being found in cultures throughout the world, a strong indicator that it has been engraved upon the hearts of all men as a part of God's natural law. This is evidenced by the fact that the understanding that hidden pre-marital sex nullifies a wedding can be found historically in different (and disconnected) cultures throughout the world:

- Every major religion to include Judaism,[65] Jainism,[66] Sikhism,[67] Christianity,[68] Islam,[69] Buddhism,[70] Hinduism,[71] Bahaism,[72] and

---

[65] The above mentioned Exodus 22:16-17 and Deuteronomy 22:28-29.

[66] "Pre-marital sex should be completely kept away. In other words, young men and young women should not engage themselves in pre-marital sex." Bhadraguptvijay *The Way Of Life: Discourses, Part 2,* (Shri Vishwakalyan Prakashan Trust, 1986), p.172.

[67] "Sikhs are forbidden to have sexual relations with anyone other than their spouse. Sikh teachings urge people to control all desires, including the sexual. The union of matrimony is considered very sacred and important, and sex outside this union is decried." The Sihk Coalition, *Common Questions About Sikhism* (http://www.khalsakids.org/Popular%20Q&A%20about%20Sikhism.pdf)

[68] "Flee fornication. Every sin that a man does is without the body; but he that commits fornication sins against his own body….Nevertheless, to avoid

39

Confucianism[73] all contain prohibitions against men and women engaging in sexual behavior before marriage.

- Under the Law of Moses a woman who concealed pre-nuptial sin from her husband to be and then had it discovered received the death penalty.[74]
- The 6th century BC Indian legal text known as the *Laws of Manu* allowed divorce for discovered pre-nuptial sin.[75]
- In Roman times it was common for men to become engaged to pre-pubescent girls as young as seven, presumably in order to ensure their virginity.[76]

---

fornication, let every man have his own wife, and let every woman have her own husband." (1Co 6:18, 7:2)

[69] "The woman and the man guilty of fornication, flog each one of them with a hundred stripes—and let not any pity for them restrain you in regard to a matter prescribed by Allah, if you believe in Allah and the Last Day, and let, some of the believers witness the punishment inflicted on them." Surah 24:2 (*Syed Maududi Translation*)

[70] "I undertake the training rule to abstain from sexual misconduct." *Five Precepts Of Buddha*, *Precept 3* (Henepola Gunaratana, *The Book Of Devotion*, Corporate Body of the Buddha Educational Foundation, 1990), p.29.

[71] "Pre-marital chastity ranks very high on the value scale of most Hindus...The major concern of Hindu society as regards sexuality is, without doubt, the preservation of female chastity...Should a girl be subjected to intercourse before marriage, the man would be expected to marry her, but in reality this did and does not always happen." Clive Lawton & Peggy Morgan *Ethical Issues In Six Religious Traditions*, (Edinburgh University Press, 2007), p.13-14.

[72] "Bahá'í law limits permissible sexual relations to those between a man and a woman in marriage. Believers are expected to abstain from sex outside matrimony." *Questions And Answers* (http://www.bahai.org/faq/)

[73] "'Is the gratifying the appetite of sex, or the doing so only according to the rules of propriety, the more important?' The answer again was, 'The observance of the rules of propriety in the matter is the more important.'" *The Works Of Mencius* Book 6: Kâo Tsze, Part 2:1:2 (James Legger, Tr., Oxford: At The Clarendon Press, 1895), p.422.

[74] Dt 22:13-21

[75] *The Laws Of Manu*, Ch. 9. No. 72, G. Buhler, Tr. *The Sacred Books Of The East*, *Vol. 25*, (Oxford: Clarendon Press, 1886), p.340.

[76] Glen Warren Bowersock, Peter Robert Lamont Brown, & Oleg Grabar, *Late Antiquity: A Guide To The Postclassical World* (Harvard University Press, 1999), p.430. Bruce W. Frier & Thomas A. J. McGinn, *A Casebook On Roman Family Law*

- In 9th century Scotland a man who deflowered a virgin without the intention of marrying her received the death penalty.[77]
- In the Fijian islands a girl who was discovered on her wedding day to not be a virgin could be killed.[78]
- In the African Bakitara tribe if it was discovered that the bride was not a virgin, her husband could send the girl back to her parents and demand the return of the marriage fee.[79]
- In the Baganda tribe the husband who discovered his bride to have concealed pre-nuptial sin would send the proof back to her parents.[80]
- In the Yoruba tribe of West Africa, upon the discovery of pre-nuptial sin after the wedding, the unchaste wife could be tied up, beaten, and forced to name her lover. If she had been betrothed to her husband as a child he had the right to send her away and demand the return of the bride-price which he had paid. Likewise, a man who took a woman's virginity was required to marry her.[81]
- In the Dahoman tribe of Africa if a bride was discovered to have committed fornication the husband could demand the return of the bride-price, together with the value of all the expenses he had incurred and the girl might be sent back to her parents. The parents would then seek to find the man who had deflowered

---

(Oxford University Press US, 2004), p.27-28. Oscar Daniel Watkins, *Holy Matrimony* (London: Rivington, Percival & Co., 1895), p.129.

[77] *The Ecclesiastical Laws Of Keneth, King of Scots, Anno 840, Can. 14-15.* Cited in Henry Virtue Tebbs, *Essay On The Scripture Doctrines Of Adultery And Divorce* (London: F.C. & J. Rivington, 1822), p.216.

[78] Thomas Williams, *Fiji And The Fijians,* (London: Hodder & Stoughton, 1870), p.144. Basil Thomson, Bolton Glanvill Corney, & James Stewart, *The Fijian: A Study Of The Decay Of Custom* (London: William Heinemann, 1908), p.201.

[79] John Roscoe, *The Bakitara, Or Banyoro* (Cambridge: University Press, 1923), p.280.

[80] John Roscoe, *The Baganda: An Account Of Their Native Customs and Beliefs,* (London: MacMillan & Co., Ltd., 1911), p.91.

[81] Samuel Johnson, *The History Of The Yorubas,* (Lagos, Nigeria: CMS Bookshops, 1921), p.114-115. E. A. Ajisafe Moore, *The Laws And Customs Of The Yoruba People* (Abeokuta, Nigeria: Fola Bookshops, no date), p.53-54. Alfred Burdon Ellis, *The Yorbua-speaking Peoples Of The Slave Coast Of West Africa,* (London: Chapman & Hall, 1894), p.183-184.

their daughter and compel him to marry her. A man who had intercourse with an unmarried woman was required to pay the bride price and take her to be his wife. If he did not want to take her as his wife he had the option of either paying a heavy fine or being enslaved (a sure deterrent to prod him into marrying the girl he had deflowered).[82]

- In the African Ashanti tribe if a husband discovered that his wife has been unchaste he could repudiate her and recover both the head money he had paid and the expenses he had incurred. A man who seduced a virgin was compelled to marry her, or, if her parents would not consent to the marriage, to pay the amount of the bride-price.[83]

- In parts of the Aztec Indian empire if a young bride was discovered to have committed pre-nuptial sin she would be publicly insulted and the husband was free to send her away if he so desired.[84]

- To the Tongans pre-nuptial chastity was so important that the groom would report it to the bride's parents and pre-nuptial sin was so discouraged in women that an elderly female relative would sometimes secretly pour blood on the sheet after the newly married couple had fell asleep in order to give the image of chastity.[85]

[82] Alfred Burdon Ellis, *The Ewe Speaking Peoples Of The Slave Coast Of West Africa*, (London: Chapman & Hall, 1890), p.156-157, 201-202. Richard Francis Burton, *Mission To Gelele, Vol. 2* (London: Tylston & Edwards, 1893), p.106-107. J. A. Skertchly, *Dahomey As It Is* (London: Chapman & Hall, 1874), p.499-500.

[83] A. B. Ellis, *The Tshi Speaking Peoples Of The Gold Coast Of West Africa* (London: Chapman & Hall, 1887), p.236-237, 282, 286.

[84] Hubert Howe Bancroft, Henry Lebbeus Oak, T. Arundel Harcourt, Albert Goldschmidt, Walter Mulrea Fisher, & William Nemos, *The Native Races Of The Pacific States Of North America, Vol. 2* (New York, NY: D. Appleton & Co., 1875), p.260-261.

[85] E. E. V. Collacott, *Marriage In Tonga* in *The Journal Of The Polynesian Society, Vol. 32, No. 128, 1923*, p.224.

- In the Samoan Islands young women would be tested before their marriages to see if they were virgins. If they were discovered to have committed pre-nuptial sin they were executed.[86]
- Amongst the Gilbert Islanders the mother of the groom would look for the blood from the rupturing of the hymen after the first intercourse. If it could not be found, the girl would be dragged outdoors naked and beaten mercilessly. As a rule, she would then be disowned from the moment when her guilt was proven and be forced into a life or prostitution (presumably because no other man would take her).[87]

Even today, in the ultra-promiscuous Western world, most men would be disappointed to discover *after* their wedding that the woman whom they had married believing to be a virgin had actually concealed a prior fornication experience from them. To this author's knowledge, there is not any culture in the world where concealed sexual behavior by the woman before the marriage would not, at the very least, be taken into consideration should the couple decide to divorce. For example, in 2008 a French court ruled that a marriage involving a woman who had lied to her husband about being a virgin was to be annulled because of her dishonesty and in some countries today women who lie about their virginity face the death penalty. The overwhelming historical and cultural support for the idea that a man and woman engaging in pre-marital sex is wrong strongly suggests that the idea that pre-nuptial sin can invalidate a wedding is a part of the moral law which God has written upon the hearts of all men.

Statistically Those Who Engage In Fornication And Then Marry Someone Else Are More Likely To Divorce

---

[86] W. T. Pritchard, *Notes On Certain Anthropological Matters Respecting The South Sea Islanders (The Samoans)* in *Publications Of The Anthropological Society Of London: Memoirs Read Before The Society, Vol. 1, 1863-1864* (London: Trubner & Co., 1865), p.324-325. George Turner, *Samoa, A Hundred Years Ago And Long Before* (London: MacMillan & Co., 1884), p.94-95.

[87] Arthur Grimble, *Migrations, Myth And Magic From The Gilbert Islands* (London: Routledge, 1972, 2004), p.68.

Not surprisingly, sociologists have now realized that women who engage in premarital sex with persons *other than* their husband to be are much more likely to end up divorcing than those who either retain their virginity until their wedding or who only have sex with their husband to be.

Joan R. Kahn, Ph.D. & Kathryn A. London, Ph.D.: "Simple cross-tabulations from the 1988 National Survey of Family Growth indicate that women who were sexually active prior to marriage faced a considerably higher risk of marital disruption than women who were virgin brides…After a variety of observable characteristics are controlled, nonvirgins still face a much higher risk of divorce than virgins."[88]

Jay Teachman, Ph.D.: "The most salient finding from this analysis is that women whose intimate premarital relationships are limited to their husbands—either premarital sex alone or premarital cohabitation—do not experience an increased risk of divorce. *It is only women who have more than one intimate premarital relationship who have an elevated risk of marital disruption.*"[89]

Daniel T. Lichter, Ph.D. & Zhenchao Qian, Ph.D.: "For serial cohabitors who married, the odds of divorce were nevertheless more than double those of women who cohabited only with their future husbands, even when controlling for past fertility and other socioeconomic characteristics."[90]

Scott T. Yabiku, Ph.D. & Mary H. Benin, Ph.D.: "Focusing on the cohabitation variables, model 1 confirms previous findings that both single cohabitors and multiple cohabitors have higher risks of divorce compared to individuals who do not cohabit before marriage, and

---

[88] *Premarital Sex And The Risk Of Divorce* in *Journal Of Marriage And Family, Vol. 53, No. 4* (November 1991), p.845.

[89] *Premarital Sex, Premarital Cohabitation, and the Risk of Subsequent Marital Dissolution Among Women* in *Journal Of Marriage And Family, Vol. 65, No. 2* (May 2003), p. 444ff.

[90] *Serial Cohabitation And The Marital Life Course* in *Journal of Marriage and Family, Vol. 70, No. 4* (November 2008), p.874.

multiple cohabitation is a greater risk factor for divorce than single cohabitation…"[91]

These are very revealing facts and they seem to confirm the basic premise of the Fornication View—*that pre-marital sex with a different partner than the one a woman marries does in some way affect a couple's marriage.* As Professor Teachman points out above, "It is only women who have more than one intimate premarital relationship who have an elevated risk of marital disruption." It is not women who only have sex with their future husbands who are at risk for a higher divorce rate but those who engage with *someone other* than their future husband. I would venture to say that the higher divorce rate for those who have committed pre-nuptial sin with someone other than their future spouse would be an outflow of the basic premise of the Fornication View. The root of these kinds of marriages failing much more often probably has more to do with these women engaging in behavior that affects their ability to enter into a wedding covenant with the man that they ultimately marry than they or the secular scientists who have studied this problem realize.

Why Is The Adultery View So Popular In American Christianity?

Any Christian who has studied the issue of divorce and remarriage will realize that the Adultery View is very popular in the United States but they may not realize why. A lot of this interpretation's popularity can be traced back to the 1960-1979 American divorce surge.

In the period between 1960 and 1979 the United States experienced an almost continual surge in the number of divorces filed each year.

---

[91] *Single and Multiple Cohabitors' Risks of Divorce*, paper presented at the annual meeting of the Population Association of America, March 31-April 2, 2005, Philadelphia, PA.

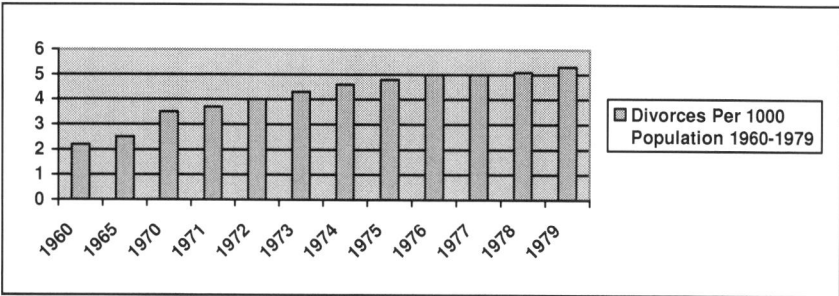

In 1960 there were only 2.2 divorces for every 1000 people in the United States. By 1970 that number had increased by 59% and before the 20 year period from the 60's to the 70's had ended the United States had experienced a *140% increase* in the number of divorces occurring.

One factor in the increase had to do with states beginning to adopt *no-fault* divorce legislation in 1953.[92] Prior to the passage of *no-fault* divorce laws a person who wanted to get a divorce had to demonstrate that the other spouse was somehow at fault in order to prove that they were "deserving" of a judge granting them a dissolution of their marriage union. These types of proof generally involved something like the commission of adultery by the other spouse or extreme abuse. But after the enacting of *no-fault* divorce it didn't matter whether one's spouse was at fault or not. A person's spouse could have been the greatest spouse in the world but if one spouse wanted a divorce there was nothing that could stop them from receiving one. It should come as no surprise that after *no-fault* legislation was enacted people were divorcing for the most trifling of reasons.

With this large increase in divorces pastors and churches were now faced with handling the growing number of individuals who had divorced and either *already had* or *desired to* remarry. Before the surge pastors had been able to focus the thrust of their divorce sermons on why a Christian should not get a divorce but now they had to address what to do if you had *already* experienced a divorce. Prior to the surge divorce

---

[92] Oklahoma was the first state in the country to adopt this type of divorce, followed by California.

and remarriage had simply just not been a pressing issue for pastors[93] and when the divorce surge began pastors were really not prepared for it theologically (you normally don't prepare for what you are not facing) and they struggled to find a theological solution for the growing number of divorces. As they looked for something that would give people guidance the Adultery View seemed to offer them a solution to the rising number of families breaking apart. Whereas the laws were beginning to allow people to divorce for any reason the Adultery View pointed people back to the old way that they needed to have a valid reason before getting a divorce and that if they went ahead and divorced anyway then they could not remarry. Pastors turning to the Adultery View in reaction to the divorce surge were probably not looking for a way to *skirt* the issue but rather to *curb* the situation. People were getting divorced just because they could and pastors who had never really faced the issue much (and therefore probably had never really thought it out before) needed a way to keep people from divorcing and remarrying and the Adultery View seemed to fit the situation. Sometimes, however, what seems to fix the situation today will create a whole new set of problems tomorrow.

Some Objections Answered

Before we look at some of the final reasons that led me to reject the Adultery View in favor of the Fornication View I would like to answer some of the objections that are often offered against the Fornication View. Many of these objections do seem plausible on the surface but the more I studied them the more I realized that under a tighter scrutiny they begin to fall apart.

Objection 1: Doesn't the Septuagint (the 2nd century BC Greek translation of the Hebrew Old Testament) use *porneia* to describe adultery?

This objection is always raised by proponents of the Adultery View. If it were true it would be a strong piece of evidence in favor of the Adultery View. This objection, however, is not true. The Septuagint does

___
[93] This is discussed more in-depth under Objection 7.

47

not use the *porneia* family of words to describe adultery but it is an *easy mistake to make* and here is why.

As noted above, the normal usage of *porneia* in Greek literature is to describe sexual behavior by single people (fornication) and because prostitutes were generally *single people engaging in sexual behavior* the word came to be used to refer to their trade. But what happens when a *married woman* becomes a full-fledged prostitute and a Greek writer wants to express this in writing? He doesn't want to emphasize her adultery because it is not the fact of her being an *adulteress* that he wants to relate but the fact that she *exchanged sexual favor in return for financial gain.* Historically, ancient Greek writers accomplished this by using the *porneia* family of words. This explains why many have mistakenly concluded that the Septuagint was using *porneia* to describe adultery because in the Septuagint there is a rather lengthy description of the Nation of Israel who is portrayed as a wife to God who has become a prostitute and her behavior is described as *porneia.* A large part of the misunderstanding over these passages has probably arose because in them Israel is portrayed as being both an *adulterer* and a *prostitute.* If a person was not familiar with the Greek usage of *porneia* they would, understandably, see it being used in the Septuagint to describe a married woman's sexual sin and assume that it was being used to describe her adultery. However, when one examines these passages carefully it becomes clear that the *porneia* family of words in the Septuagint is being used to describe the *prostituting* nature of Israel's behavior, not her *adultery.* This can be easily demonstrated by just looking at the passages.

Israel Described As A Wife Who Has Become A Prostitute	Scripture Passages Illustrating This
In these passages Israel is referred to as a young woman whom God meets and enters into a "covenant" with to become his wife.	"And I passed by you and saw you, and behold, your season was a season of lodgers, and I spread my wings over you and covered your disgrace, and I swore to you and entered into a covenant with you,

	says the Lord, and you became mine." Ezek 16:8NETS[94]
After the wedding God causes His wife to prosper and become beautiful.	"And I bathed you with water and washed your blood from you and anointed you with oil, and I clothed you with embroidered clothes and shod you with blue and girded you with fine linen and clothed you in a fine hair-veil, and I adorned you with an ornament and put bracelets around your arms and a chain around your neck, and I gave an earring on your nostril and small rings on your ears and a crown of boasting upon your head. And you were adorned with gold and silver, and your wraps were of fine linen and of woven hair and embroidered. You ate choice flour and oil and honey, and you became very beautiful." Ezek 16:9-13NETS
After being made beautiful and prosperous, God's wife realizes that the prosperity given to her by her Husband has made her valuable in the eyes of other men.	"And your fame went out among the nations on account of your beauty, because you had been completed in attractiveness by the elegance that I set upon you…And you trusted in your beauty…" Ezek 16:14-15NETS
Realizing her value to other men she begins to sell herself sexually to, not just a few men but, *a large*	"You built your brothel (*porneion*) at every head of a road, and you made your pedestal in every boulevard,

---

[94] The idea of a husband and wife type relationship between God and Israel are also typified in Isaiah 54:5, Jeremiah 3:1, 20 and Hosea 1:2. See also Ephesians 5:25-32.

number of people.	and <u>you became like a whore</u> <u>(*porne*) gathering payments</u>." Ezek 16:31NETS "And you have played the whore (*ek-porneuo*) with <u>many shepherds</u>, and would you return to me?" Jer 3:1cNETS "And you trusted in your beauty, and you whored (*porneuo*) because of your fame and poured out your whoring (*porneia*) <u>on every passer-by</u>." Ezek 16:15NETS "...you also built for yourself a whoring (*pornikon*) chamber, and you made a proclamation for yourself in <u>every boulevard</u>. And <u>at the head of every way</u> you built your whorehouses (*porneia*), and you spoiled your beauty and drew your legs apart for <u>every passer-by</u> and multiplied your whoring (*porneia*)." Ezek 16:24-25NETS "...and you played the whore (*ek-porneuo*) <u>frequently</u> so as to provoke me." Ezek 16:26NETS
In fact, she becomes so engrossed in prostitution that she is described as an individual that can never be satisfied, no matter how much prostitution she is able to get.	"And you played the whore (*ek-porneuo*) with daughters of Assour, and even so you <u>were not satisfied</u>, and you played the whore (*ek-porneuo*) but <u>were not satiated</u>. And you multiplied your covenants with the land of the Chaldeans, and you <u>were not even satisfied</u> with them." Ezek 16:28-29NETS
She becomes so infatuated with the profession of prostitution that she	"...you also <u>built for yourself a</u> <u>whoring (*pornikon*) chamber</u>, and

even goes so far as to build a number of houses of prostitution just to sell her services.	you made a proclamation for yourself in every boulevard..." Ezek 16:24NETS "You built your brothel (*porneion*) at every head of a road..." Ezek 16:31NETS "And I will give you over into their hands, and they shall eradicate your brothel (*porneion*), and they shall demolish your pedestal..." Ezek 16:39NETS
By engaging in this kind of behavior she is certainly guilty of committing *adultery* because she had sexual relations with someone while she was married to someone else.	"And I saw that for everything in which the settlement of Israel was caught, [in which she committed adultery (*moichao*)], and I sent her away and gave her a document of dismissal..." Jer 3:8NETS "...for they were committing adultery (*moichao*) and blood was on their hands; they were committing adultery (*moichao*) with their notions and they drove their children that they bore me through flames to them." Ezek 23:37NETS
But she is also guilty of *prostitution* because she sold herself sexually to these individuals.	"...you did all these things, deeds of a woman of whoredom (*porne*)...you played the whore (*ek-porneuo*) three times with your daughters...you became like a whore (*porne*) gathering payments." Ezek 16:30-31NETS "...and I will turn you back from whoring (*porneia*)..." Ezek 16:41NETS "And they were entering into her; as they enter into a whoring woman

	(porne), so they were entering into Oola and Ooliba to commit lawlessness." Ezek 23:44NETS
	"For from the wages of whoredom (porneia) she gathered them, and from the wages of whoredom (porne) she brought them together." Mic 1:7d-eNETS
	"…and they shall become weak in their bodies, because of a multitude of whoredom (porneia). Beautiful and gratifying prostitute (porne), manipulator of potions, she who barters nations through her whoredom (porneia) and tribes through her potions." Nah 3:3-4NETS
In effect she has become _both_ an adulterer and a prostitute and in the end God makes it clear that her sins are both adultery _and_ prostitution.	"Therefore I said, Do they not commit adultery (moicheuo) with these? and has she _also_ gone a-whoring (ek-porneuo) after the manner of a harlot (porne)?" Ezek 23:43Brenton
	"Contend against your mother, contend—for she is not my wife, and I am not her husband—and I will put away her whoring (porneia) from before me _and_ her adultery (moicheia) from between her breasts…" Hos 2:2NETS
	"And her whoredom (porneia) came to nothing, _and_ she committed adultery (moicheuo) with tree and stone." Jer 3:9NETS

After reviewing these passages it becomes clear that the *porneia* family of words is not being used to describe the *adulterous* nature of

Israel's behavior but rather the *prostituting* nature of her behavior. She is not guilty of *pornea* because she committed adultery. She is guilty of *pornea* because she engaged in prostitution.

Understanding that *pornea* can be used to describe prostitution, even in the case of a married woman, will now help to explain another passage from the Septuagint that is sometimes brought forward as evidence that *pornea* can mean adultery.

> **So it is with a woman who leaves her husband and provides an heir <u>by a stranger</u>. For first of all, she has disobeyed the law of the Most High; second, she has committed an offense against her husband; and third, she has committed adultery (*moicheuo*) through harlotry (*pornea*) and brought forth children by another man. She herself will be brought before the assembly, and punishment will fall on her children. 23:22-24RSV**

Some have looked at this passage and concluded that it is using *pornea* to describe a woman who has entered into an adulterous relationship, the result of which was a child. At first glance this does seem plausible, however a closer examination of the passage shows that this is not the case and that this passage actually is in support of the thesis that *pornea* carries with it the idea of prostitution and here is why. We have in this passage a woman who gets pregnant by "a stranger". The Greek word for stranger is *allotrios*. It is the same Greek word that we find used in John 10:5 where Jesus states, "And a stranger (*allotrios*) will they not follow, but will flee from him: for they know not the voice of strangers (*allotrios*)." The implication is that this woman had intercourse with a person that she did not know. The kind of behavior engaged in by this woman is not that of a wife who falls in love with another man and then enters into an adulterous relationship with him. This is a woman who *does not know* the individual (he is a stranger) but engages in willful intercourse with him anyway. This description perfectly fits a wife who has decided to engage in prostitution for financial gain. This is reflected in the above translation where her behavior is described as one who "has committed adultery ***through harlotry*** (*pornea*)." She is not an adulterer just because she committed *pornea* (prostitution) but in her *pornea* (prostitution) she became an adulterer. Further proof of this being a case of a woman involved in prostitution is found in the way that her

53

illegitimate child is treated. The passage indicates that "punishment will fall upon her children." This is because, according to the Law of Moses, "One born of a harlot shall not enter into the assembly of the Lord".[95] The children of prostitutes were ostracized and cast out from ancient Israeli society. The punishment of this woman's children is exactly what one would expect to occur to the children of a woman who had become involved in *prostitution*.

After careful examination the Septuagint passages that are often presented as evidence that *porneia* means adultery actually show just the opposite. The understanding that *porneia* does not mean adultery can be seen even clearer in the Old Testament in passages that were clearly involving adultery. As noted above there are three related Hebrew words for adultery and they appear 34 times in the Hebrew Old Testament. Yet in none of these cases was the word *porneia* chosen by the Septuagint translators to translate any of them. Even in the Old Testament's most famous case of adultery, that between David and Bathsheba, the word *porneia* is not used to describe their behavior.[96] One would think that if *porneia* did carry with it the meaning of adultery in pre-New Testament times that in at least one of these clear instances in the Old Testament that it would have been used to translate it. Yet we never find the Septuagint translators doing so. And if one has any doubt as to the Septuagint's usage of *porneia* all they need to do is look up each verse that uses *porneia* and it will be obvious that it is never used to refer clearly to adultery.[97]

---

[95] Deut 23:2LXXBrenton

[96] 2Sam 11:4LXX

[97] All one need do is merely look up each of the references in the Septuagint (which is available on various websites) along with an inter-linear Septuagint and one will see that *porneia* is not used for adultery. The references, per *A Handy Concordance of the Septuagint* (London: S. Bagster & Sons, 1887) and *Wiki Lexicon Of The Greek New Testament And Concordance* (http://lexicon.katabiblon.com, 2011), are as follows: **Porneia:** Gen 38:24, Num 14:33, 2Ki 9:22, Is 47:10, 57:9, Jer 2:20, 3:2, 3:9, 13:27, Eze 16:15, 16:22, 16:25, 16:33, 16:34, 16:36, 16:41, 23:7, 23:8(2), 23:11(2), 23:14, 23:17, 23:18, 23:19, 23:27, 23:29(2), 23:35, 43:7, 43:9, Hos 1:2(2), 2:2, 2:4, 4:11, 4:12, 5:4, 6:10, Mic 1:7(2), Nah 3:3, 3:4, Sir 23:23, 26:9, 41:17, Tob 4:12, 8:7, Wis Sol 14:12. **Porneion:** Eze 16:25, 16:31, 16:39. **Porneuo:** Deu 23:17, Jdg 2:15, 1Ch 5:25, Ps 72:27, 105:39, Jer 3:6, 3:7, 3:8, Eze 6:9, 16:15, 16:34, 23:3, 23:19, Hos 3:3, 4:10, 4:14, 4:17, 9:1, Amo 7:17. **Porne:** Gen 34:31, 38:15, 38:21(2), 38:22, Lev 21:7, 21:14, Deu 23:2, 23:17, 23:18, Jos 2:1, 6:17, 6:23, 6:25, Jdg 11:1, 16:1, 1Ki 3:16,

54

Objection 2: Didn't God divorce his wife Israel because she committed adultery?

Another objection that is often raised is the issue of God divorcing his unfaithful wife Israel in Jeremiah 3:6-14 because of her adultery.

> The LORD said also to me in the days of Josiah the king: "Have you seen what backsliding Israel has done? She has gone up on every high mountain and under every green tree, and there played the harlot. And I said, after she had done all these *things,* 'Return to Me.' But she did not return. And her treacherous sister Judah saw it. Then I saw that <u>for all the causes for which backsliding Israel had committed adultery, I had put her away and given her a certificate of divorce</u>; yet her treacherous sister Judah did not fear…Return, backsliding Israel,' says the LORD; 'I will not cause My anger to fall on you. For I *am* merciful,' says the LORD; 'I will not remain angry forever. Only acknowledge your iniquity, That you have transgressed against the LORD your God, and have scattered your charms to alien deities under every green tree, And you have not obeyed My voice,' says the LORD. "Return, O backsliding children," says the LORD; "<u>for I am married to you</u>. I will take you, one from a city and two from a family, and I will bring you to Zion." NKJV

At face value this objection does seem to be in favor of the Adultery View but upon closer examination one will realize that in reality it actually is teaching against the idea that a divorce for adultery dissolves the marriage covenant. In the above passage Israel is presented as the wife of God who has committed adultery. Finally, her spurned husband

---

12*p*24*l*8, 20:19, 22:38, Pro 5:3, 6:26, 29:3, Is 1:21, 23:15, 23:16, 57:3, Jer 3:3, 5:7, Eze 16:30, 16:31, 16:35, 23:43, 23:44, Hos 4:14(2), Joe 3:3, Nah 3:4, Sir 9:6, 19:2, EpJer 1:9, PsSol 2:11. **Pornikos:** Pr 7:10, Eze 16:24. **Pornokopos:** Pr 23:21. **Ekporneuo:** Gen 38:24, Ex 34:15, 34:16, Lev 17:7, 19:29(2), 20:5, 20:6, 21:9, Num 15:39, 25:1, Deu 22:21, 31:16, Jdg 2:17, 8:27, 8:33, 2Ch 21:11, 21:13(2), Pr 24:11, Jer 3:1, Ezk 6:9(2), 16:16, 16:17, 16:20, 16:26(2), 16:27, 16:28(2), 16:30, 16:33, 20:30, 23:3, 23:5, 23:30, 23:43, Hos 1:2(2), 2:5, 4:12, 4:13, 4:18, 5:3, Sir 46:11. **Pornos:** Hos 4:14, Jer 5:7, Sir 23:17(2), PsSol 2:11.

has enough and explains that because "Israel had committed adultery, I had put her away and given her a certificate of divorce". Yet, look at what God says at the end of the passage *after* he has divorced his wife for adultery. He indicates that even though she has committed adultery and even though he has obtained a legal divorce from her he still acknowledges that "*I am married to you.*" You see, despite her adultery and her being given a certificate of divorce, in God's eyes *she was still his wife*. God did not proceed to look for another wife. Instead he tried to woo her back saying "*Return, backsliding Israel...Return...*"

Under the Law of Moses adultery is never given as a reason for divorcing and remarrying. And this fact, coupled with how God reacts to his adulterous wife in this passage, is very strong evidence that God does not view adultery as having actually dissolved the marriage. By his own admission, his legally divorced and adulterous wife was still His wife *after* the divorce. The plain truth of the matter is that adultery then did not, nor does it now, dissolve a marriage.

Objection 3: Doesn't the Apostle Paul use *porneia* to describe the ancient Israelis committing adultery?

In the book of 1Corinthians a passage has been suggested by supporters of the Adultery View as proof that *porneia* carried with it the idea of adultery. That passage is 1Corinthians 10:1-8 where it states:

> Moreover, brethren, I would not that you should be ignorant, how that all our fathers were under the cloud, and all passed through the sea...But with many of them God was not well pleased: for they were overthrown in the wilderness. Now these things were our examples, to the intent we should not lust after evil things, as they also lusted...Neither let us commit fornication (*porneuo*), as some of them committed, and in one day twenty three thousand fell.

This passage is a reference to Num 25:1-9 which details the ancient Israelis who engaged in sexual relations with Moabite women. Like another passage which we will look at, it is used to support the Adultery View based upon an *assumption*. Supporters of the Adultery View maintain that it is safe to *assume* that at least some of the 20,000 people who died as a result of committing *porneuo* (actually it was 20,000 in just

56

one day, the end total was 24,000) surely must have been married and therefore *porneuo* was used to describe adulterous behavior. There are two major problems with this interpretation. First, the Bible nowhere says (either in Numbers or 1Corinthians) that the people were married and it's not safe to base a doctrine upon an *assumption* when you do not have proof for it. And secondly, there is strong evidence in the book of Numbers to imply that these were *single* people. That evidence is based upon a census that is recorded in the chapter following the above incident.

> **And it came to pass after the plague, that the LORD spoke unto Moses and unto Eleazar the son of Aaron the priest, saying, Take the sum of all the congregation of the children of Israel, from twenty years old and upward, throughout their fathers' house, all that are able to go to war in Israel…These were the numbered of the children of Israel, six hundred thousand and a thousand seven hundred and thirty…And these are they that were numbered of the Levites after their families…And those that were numbered of them were twenty and three thousand, all males from a month old and upward: for they were not numbered among the children of Israel, because there was no inheritance given them among the children of Israel. Num 26:1-2, 51, 57, 62**

According to the census there were 601,730 males twenty years and older, excluding those who were too old or ill to go to war and the Levites (who were counted in a second census which included all male children one month and older and totaled 23,000). For statistical purposes we can use the 601,730 men and compare that with the 24,000 fornicators who died. Factoring in the 24,000 fornicating men who died right before the census was taken gives a census total of 625,730. 24,000 men out of a total population of 625,730 equal only 3.8% of the population who are recorded as having committed fornication and died as a result. The actual percentage would be less than 3.8 because of the census of the Levites for which it does not indicate how many sexually mature males there were. Is it hard to believe that there were as many as 3.8% of the male population who were unmarried? Not really, when in the United States

18.24 percent of all adult men have never been married.[98] Far from proving that *porneuo* carries with it the idea of adultery the only thing that this passage proves is that it is unsafe to make assumptions when it comes to the meaning of *porneia*.

Objection 4: Doesn't the Apostle Paul use *porneia* to describe an adulterous relationship in 1Corinthians 5:1?

In his first letter to the Corinthians Paul writes that:

It is reported commonly that there is fornication (*porneia*) among you, and such fornication (*porneia*) as is not so much as named among the Gentiles, that one should have his father's wife.

In this passage a male individual is rebuked for having a sexual relationship with his step-mother. Advocates of the Adultery View have pointed to this passage and said that it offered proof that *porneia* at the time of the New Testament did indeed carry with it the idea of adultery. They maintain that the father is still alive and therefore how could this not be a situation where *porneia* is being used to describe adultery. The entire argument as to whether this verse is a proof passage that *porneia* can be used to refer to adultery hinges on whether the father is alive or not. The main reason for assuming that he was alive is 2Corinthians 7:12 where Paul writes, "Wherefore, though I wrote unto you, I did it not for his cause that had done the wrong, nor for his cause that suffered wrong..." Advocates of the Adultery View maintain that the one who had "suffered wrong" was the still living father but there are a number of reasons for rejecting this conclusion and assuming that the father is dead. First, it would involve assigning a meaning to *porneia* (that of adultery) for which I have already demonstrated would have been against its normal usage. Paul's choice of *porneia* to describe these two people's behavior would seem to indicate that the father was dead. It was not adultery (*moicheia*) that the son was said to be committing, but fornication

---

98 Women's Voices, Women's Vote, *"The State of Unmarried America: A Demographic, Lifestyle, and Attitudinal Overview of America's Emerging Majority,"* February 2006, p.14.

(*porneia*). Secondly, scholars are divided as to who the one who "suffered wrong" was with various interpreters identifying it as the Apostle Paul,[99] the entire Christian Community at Corinth,[100] the family of the incestuous person,[101] or the deceased father of the son.[102] If the passage is referring to the father (which I believe it very well could be) it does not absolutely mean that he was still living. As Dr. Adam Clarke points out "these words might be spoken in reference to the father, if dead, whose cause should be vindicated; as his injured honor might be considered, like Abel's blood, to be crying from the earth."[103] Finally, there is even disagreement over how to best translate the passage with some Greek experts suggesting that instead of translating it "suffered wrong" it should read "the wrong done"[104] which would make it read:

Wherefore, though I wrote unto you, I did it not for his cause who had done the wrong, nor on account of <u>the wrong done</u>, but that our care for you in the sight of God might appear unto you.[105]

Regardless of the correct way to translate this passage it is poor scholarship to allow an *unclear passage* to define a word (which is what the Adultery View is doing here). If all of the evidence points towards the Adultery View I do not see why those who support it have to resort to an *unclear passage* to back up their argument. One would think that if the Adultery View was true then there would be plenty of *clear* New Testament verses to back it up. Common sense tells us to define this

---

[99] Robert E. Picirilli, *Randall House Bible Commentary Series: 1 & 2 Corinthians* (Nashville, TN: Randall House Publishers, 1987), p.351.

[100] Johann Albrecht Bengel, *Gnomon Of The New Testament, Vol. 3* (Edinburgh: T&T Clark, 1858), p.398.

[101] Adam Clarke notes this interpretation in *Clarke's Commentary: The New Testament, Vol. 7* (Albany, OR: Ages, 1997), p.803.

[102] Adam Clarke, *Clarke's Commentary: The New Testament, Vol. 7* (Albany, OR: Ages, 1997), p.803.

[103] Adam Clarke, *Clarke's Commentary: The New Testament, Vol. 7* (Albany, OR: Ages, 1997), p.803.

[104] Gustav Billroth, *A Commentary On The Epistles Of Paul To The Corinthians, Vol. 2* (Edinburgh: Thomas Clark, 1838), p.269-271.

[105] Duncan Convers, *Marriage And Divorce In The United States: As They Are And As They Ought To Be* (J. B. Lippincott Co., 1889), p.209.

unclear passage by the general usage of the word which we demonstrated was pre-marital sex and as such a more likely scenario would be as follows:

In Roman times it was common for men to marry much younger women. In the above case a man who had children from a previous relationship ended up marrying a much younger woman who was about the same age as his son. Things went on this way for a while and then one day the father died. Now you just had the step-mother and the step-son, both about the same age, living in the same house together. Gradually, as these two people who are both single and about the same age, see each other every day they begin to develop feelings for each other. Maybe the step-son strongly resembles his father and this reminds the grieving widow of her deceased husband. One thing leads to another and before you know it these two people have fell in love and began to engage in a physical, romantic relationship.

This type of scenario perfectly fits with what we know about Roman marriage customs wherein young women were often married to older men. In Paul's day it was such a common occurrence for young women to have been widowed that Paul had to create special rules for dealing with it in regards to the church's welfare program.[106] If the situation here had been one of an adulterous relationship Paul would have dealt with it by discussing the issue of divorce and remarriage, something that he does two chapters later without making the smallest reference to the step-son/step-mother situation which would imply that it had nothing to do with adultery. As mentioned above this passage is used by the proponents of the Adultery View based upon the *assumption* that the father is alive, although there is no clear evidence in the New Testament to indicate that he was. Logic and wisdom teach us that we cannot make a decision that has the potential to send someone to hell for

---

[106] "But the **younger widows** refuse: for when they have begun to wax wanton against Christ, they will marry; having damnation, because they have cast off their first faith. And withal they learn to be idle, wandering about from house to house; and not only idle, but tattlers also and busybodies, speaking things which they ought not. I will therefore that the younger women marry, bear children, guide the house, give none occasion to the adversary to speak reproachfully." (1Tim 5:11-14)

60

all eternity based upon an *assumption*. Based on the general usage of *porneia* by Greek writers one can safely conclude that Paul's decision to use this word to describe the behavior between these two people, rather than the Greek word for adultery (*moicheia*) is evidence that it was fornication (sexual behavior by two single people)[107] that was the issue here.

Objection 5: Didn't God divorce Israel and marry the Church?

There are those who have tried to maintain that eventually God did divorce Israel and married the Gentile church in her place. This is a misinterpretation for a number of reasons. First, the church never replaced Israel as God's wife. Instead the church became a part of Israel. In the book of Ephesians 2:11-3:6 the Apostle Paul explained to his Gentile readers that prior to their becoming Christians they were "without Christ, being aliens from the commonwealth of Israel and strangers from the covenants of promise, having no hope, and without God in the world: But now…therefore you are no more strangers and foreigners, but fellow-citizens [of Israel]…" He explained that through Christ's work on earth He "has made both [Jews and Gentiles] one, and has broken down the middle wall of partition between us; having abolished in his flesh the enmity, even the law of commandments contained in ordinances; so that in Himself He might make the two into one new man, so making peace; and that he might reconcile both unto God in one body by the cross…" In fact, Paul maintained that his whole ministry to the Gentiles was based upon the fact that God had "made known unto me the mystery…That the Gentiles should be fellow heirs [with the Jews], and of the same body, and partakers of his promise in Christ by the gospel."

The nation of Israel was made up of the descendants of Abraham and Paul explained to the Christians in Galatia that now "it is those who are of faith who are sons of Abraham…There is neither Jew nor Greek…for you are all one in Christ Jesus. And if you belong to Christ, then you are Abraham's descendants, heirs according to promise (Gal 3:7, 28-29NASB)."

---

[107] And that of a grosser nature.

In order to explain this concept better Paul used the illustration of a cultivated olive tree that had a branch from a wild olive tree grafted into it:

But if some of the branches were broken off, and you, being a wild olive, were grafted in among them and became partaker with them of the rich root of the olive tree, do not be arrogant toward the branches; but if you are arrogant, remember that it is not you who supports the root, but the root supports you. You will say then, "Branches were broken off so that I might be grafted in." Quite right, they were broken off for their unbelief, but you stand by your faith. Do not be conceited, but fear; for if God did not spare the natural branches, He will not spare you, either. Behold then the kindness and severity of God; to those who fell, severity, but to you, God's kindness, if you continue in His kindness; otherwise you also will be cut off. And they also, if they do not continue in their unbelief, will be grafted in, for God is able to graft them in again. For if you were cut off from what is by nature a wild olive tree, and were grafted contrary to nature into a cultivated olive tree, how much more will these who are the natural branches be grafted into their own olive tree? Ro 11:17-24NASB

And according to Paul, all who had experienced a new birth heart change were Jewish, and therefore all Christians were a part of the Jewish nation now:

For he is not a Jew, which is one outwardly; neither is that circumcision, which is outward in the flesh: But he is a Jew, which is one inwardly; and circumcision is that of the heart, in the spirit, and not in the letter; whose praise is not of men, but of God. Ro 2:28-29

So, God did not divorce his wife Israel to marry the church, rather he allowed a people group (the Gentiles) to become a part of Israel.

Objection 6: Some of the Greek dictionaries that I have say that one of the definitions of *porneia* is adultery, so how could the exception clause not be referring to adultery?

This is probably one of the most confusing aspects of this issue because even dictionaries seem to disagree on how to define *porneia*. Some define it as sexual immorality (which would include adultery) but others define it as fornication (which carries with it the idea of pre-marital sex). Here are photocopies from twelve Greek-English dictionaries which define *porneia* as either fornication or prostitution (a profession generally entered into by *single persons who commit fornication for a living*). Note that these dictionaries use the Greek characters so *porneia* will be written as either Πορνεία or πορνεία:

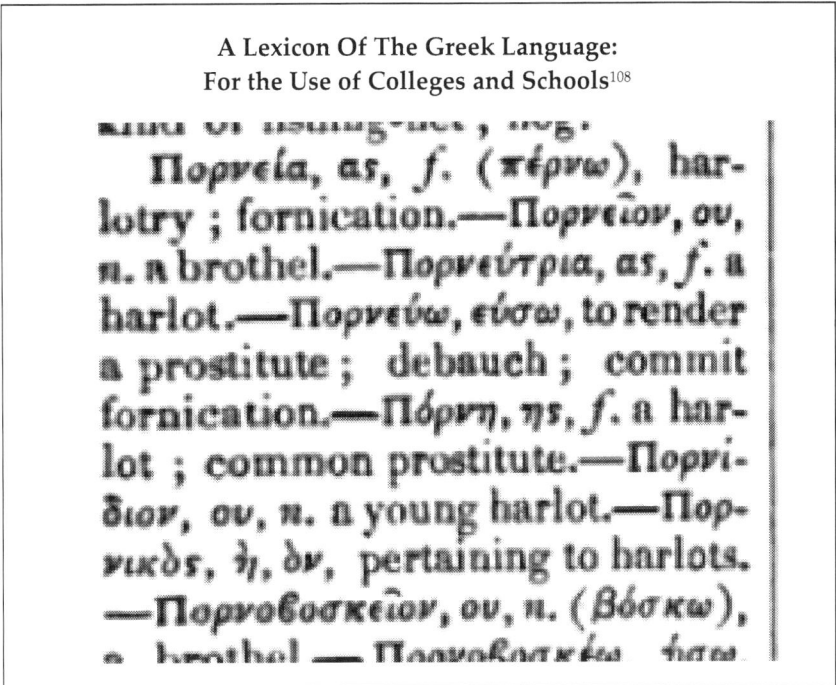

A Lexicon Of The Greek Language:
For the Use of Colleges and Schools[108]

Πορνεία, ας, *f.* (πέρνω), harlotry ; fornication.—Πορνεῖον, ου, *n.* a brothel.—Πορνεύτρια, ας, *f.* a harlot.—Πορνεύω, εύσω, to render a prostitute ; debauch ; commit fornication.—Πόρνη, ης, *f.* a harlot ; common prostitute.—Πορνίδιον, ου, *n.* a young harlot.—Πορνικός, ἡ, ὄν, pertaining to harlots.—Πορνοβοσκεῖον, ου, *n.* (βόσκω), a brothel.— Πορνοβοσκέω, ήσω.

---

[108] John Allen Giles, (London: Longman, Orme, Brown, Green, and Longmans, 1840)

A Greek-English Lexicon: Based On
The German Work Of Francis Passow[109]

Πορνεία, ας, ἡ, (πορνεύω) *fornica-tion*, Dem. 403, 26, etc.
Πορνεῖον, ου, τό, *a house of ill fame*,

An English-Greek Lexicon[110]

Formidably, δεινῶς, Omn.
Fornication, πορνεία, Dem.
To forsake, λείπω, Omn. ; ἐγκαταλείπω, P.

---

[109] Henry George Liddell, Robert Scott, & Henry Drisler, (New York: Harper & Brothers, 1846)

[110] Charles Duke Yonge, (London: Longman, Brown, Green, and Longmans, 1849)

Greek Lexicon Of The Roman And
Byzantine Periods From B.C. 146 To A.D. 1100[111]

Αnust. Sm. 1012 C.

πορνεία, ας, ἡ, (πορνεύω) *fornication.* Classical. | π
Sept. Gen. 38, 24. Tobit 8, 7. *Paul. Cor.*
1, 7, 2 (*Method.* 77 C Διὰ τὴν ἀνάγκην τῆς
πορνείας). — **2.** *Intercourse with the gentiles ;*
idolatry. A Hebraism. *Sept.* Num. 14, 33. | π
Hos. 1, 2. 2, 2, et alibi.

πορνεύω, *to commit fornication.* *Sept.* Deut. 23,

An English-Greek Lexicon:
Containing All The Words In General Use[112]

Formless, ἄμορφος

Fornication, πορνεία, *f* : to commit
  fornication, πορνεύω
Fornicator, πόρνος, *m.*   [ἵσταμαι

A New Greek And English Lexicon[113]

Πορνεία, ας, ἡ, harlotry ; fornication. *Th.* πόρνη.
(Πορνεῖον, ου, τὸ, a brothel.

---

[111] Evangelinus Apostolides Sophocles, (New York: Charles Scribner's Sons, 1900)
[112] Henry R. Hamilton, (London: John Weale, 1855)
[113] James Donnegan, (London: J. F. Dove, 1831)

A Greek-English Lexicon: Containing All The Words In General Use[114]

Πορνεία, ας, ƒ. fornication

Πορνεῖον, ου, n. brothel

Greek-English Lexicon To The New Testament After the Latest and Best Authorities[115]

1 Tim. vi. 5, 6.
πορνεία, ἡ, *fornication*, Matt. xv. 19. Acts, xv. 20, 29. 1 Cor. vi. 18 ; met., *idolatry*, Rev. ii. 21. xiv. 8. xvii. 2, 4.
πορνεύω, *to commit fornication*,

---

[114] Henry R. Hamilton, (London: Lockwood & Co., 1871)
[115] W. J. Hickie, (New York: The MacMillan Co., 1911)

A Critical Greek And English
Concordance Of The New Testament To
Which Is Added Green's Greek And English Lexicon[116]

πορνεία.

fornication, Matt. v. 32. xv. 19. xix. 9. Mark vii. 21. John viii. 41. Acts xv. 20, 29. xxi. 25. Rom. i. 29(*om S*). 1 Cor. v. 1*l*. vi. 13, 18. vii. 2. 2 Cor. xii. 21. Gal. v. 19. Eph. v. 3. Col. iii. 5. 1 Thes. iv. 3. Rev. ii. 21. ix. 21. xiv. 8. xvii. 2, 4. xviii. 3. xix. 2.

Add Rev. xvii. 5, for πόρνη, C^m.

πορνεύω.

An Intermediate Greek-English Lexicon[117]

of the spearhead and shaft, II.
πορνεία, ἡ, *fornication, prostitution*, Dem.
πορνεῖον, τό, *a house of ill-fame, brothel*, Ar.
πορνεύω, *to prostitute* :—Pass., of a woman, *to be or become a prostitute*, Hdt., Dem., etc.   II. intr. in Act., = Pass., Luc.   From

---

[116] Charles Frederic Hudson, Ezra Abbot, Thomas Sheldon Green, (Boston: H. L. Hastings, 1885)
[117] Henry George Liddell & Robert Scott, (Oxford: Clarendon Press, 1900)

practise idolatry, Kev. 2. 14.
πορνεία, ας, fornication, Mat. 5. 32.
πορνείον, ου, a brothel, Ran. 113.

A Lexicon Of New Testament Greek, On A New Plan[119]

18 πορνεία, n., *fornication.*
    πορνείᾳ,   D. S.
    πορνείαι,   N. P.
    πορνείαν,   A. S.
    πορνείας, G. S. & A. P.   (18)
19 πορνεύω, v., *to commit fornication.*
20 πόρνη, n., *a harlot, a whore*

In a previous section we have demonstrated that the general usage of *porneia* was to refer to something that was *different than adultery* (i.e. fornication) and the above twelve dictionaries support this view. Why, then, do some dictionaries define *porneia* as if it was a catch all phrase for sexual immorality? The answer to this question is two-fold.

The first reason that some dictionaries present *porneia* as a catch all phrase for sexual immorality is referred to as "circular reasoning". Many people have interpreted the exception clause to be referring to adultery. They say that Jesus *is* making an exception *for adultery*; therefore whatever Greek word is used *must mean* adultery. But this way of interpreting a Greek word is completely backwards. You do not interpret a Greek word by what you *think* the verse is saying, you interpret the verse by what the Greek word is, based upon its normal usage in other literature (which in this case strongly suggests it to be something different than adultery).

---

[118] John Jones, (London: Longman, Hurst, Rees, Orme, Brown, and Green, 1825)
[119] Theodore Jones, (London: Elliot Stock, 1877)

Secondly, a lot of confusion has come in because of *porneia*'s usage to describe prostitution (which, as noted above, is normally a profession in which single, unmarried women engage in sexual behavior). The confusion comes in when it is used to describe a married woman who chooses to become a prostitute. Misunderstanding its usage in the Septuagint to describe the prostituting nature of the nation of Israel as God's wife has largely been responsible for giving rise to the idea that it means adultery.

I realize that this is going to be one of the harder objections to persuade people's minds on because we have the understanding that *"dictionaries do not make mistakes"*. After all, we go to dictionaries when we want to have the *final and undisputed* answer as to what a word means. What makes this situation unique, though, is that it is not a situation where all dictionaries agree on what is the final and undisputed answer — *it is a situation where dictionaries are in disagreement and we are trying to discern which definition is correct.* I realize that it can be hard to accept that some of the resources which we have relied upon as being the final authorities may have inaccuracies but the reality is that dictionaries do make mistakes. When Noah Webster was creating what would become the famous "Webster's Dictionary" he wrote that there were *"principal defects in all our dictionaries; it occurs in almost every page, defeating, in a great degree, the object of such works"*[120] One of the reasons that he created his dictionary was because he found the dictionaries available to him to be very defective and he wanted to produce something better. And it was not just dictionaries in Webster's day that made mistakes. To show how easy it is for a dictionary to make a mistake we need only point to a definition mistake that the world's premier English dictionary has made for *ninety nine years*. The *Oxford English Dictionary* is considered to be the most accurate English dictionary that has ever been created. Its own website claims that it is *"regarded as the accepted authority on the English language"*, that it is *"the most complete record of the English language ever assembled"* and that it is an *"unsurpassed guide to the meaning, history, and pronunciation"* of the English language. Yet, despite such claims of robustness, for nearly one hundred years it has carried a wrong definition

---

[120] *A Compendious Dictionary Of The English Language* (New-Haven: Sidney's Press, 1806), Preface

for the word "siphon" and the story of its discovery helps to shed a little light on how dictionary mis-entries occur.

In 2010 Dr. Stephen Hughes, a physics professor at the Queensland University of Technology, was writing a paper about siphons (the tubes that are used to move liquid from one place to another and which commonly used to transfer gasoline out of a car's gas tank into another container). As a physicist Dr. Hughes knew that siphons worked because of gravity but that there was the common misconception that it was atmospheric pressure which made them work. As he researched for his paper he was discouraged to find that even the *Oxford English Dictionary* promoted this misconception defining a siphon as a tube *"used for drawing off liquids by means of atmospheric pressure"*. In his search for a correct dictionary entry Dr. Hughes relates that:

> **An extensive check of online and offline dictionaries did not reveal a single dictionary that correctly referred to gravity being the operative force in a siphon. The author checked the entire collection of dictionaries in the Queensland University of Technology library...Over 25 online dictionaries were checked (see appendix) and not a single definition referred to gravity as the operative force in a siphon.**[121]

Apparently, what had happened was that one dictionary made the mistake and others followed in suit, including *"the accepted authority on the English language"*.[122] When a staff person from the *Oxford English Dictionary* (OED) was asked about the mistake their answer presented more questions than it did solutions. They indicated that "The OED entry for siphon dates from 1911 and was written by editors who were not scientists".[123] That is very revealing because it indicates that even in what is considered to be the best dictionary in the English speaking world,

---

[121] Stephen W. Hughes, *A Practical Example Of A Siphon At Work* in *Physics Education Journal, Vol. 45, No. 2* (March 2010), p.162-166.

[122] I was able to trace the mistake back as far as the entry in the 1881 edition of *Knight's American Mechanical Dictionary, Vol. 3,* (Boston: Houghton, Mifflin & Co.), p.2188, entry for siphon.

[123] Lewis Page, *Physicist Unmasks 99-Year-Old Mistake In English Dictionaries* http://www.theregister.co.uk/2010/05/10/siphon_dictionary_error/ accessed March 1, 2011.

some of the people who wrote it were not even qualified to write about what they did and ended up misleading people for a hundred years. And as surprising as I am sure that this will be to some people, it really shouldn't surprise us. Even Noah Webster did not claim infallibility. *After* publishing one of the first editions of his now famous dictionary he admitted in relation to the criticism that he had laid on his predecessors that, *"From the censure implied in this remark, I am not myself wholly free..."*[124] and, hence, he came out with a *revised* edition of his dictionary because he felt that the previous one he had written contained *errors*.

And all this brings us back to our original question as to why some dictionaries define porneia as *adultery*. The answer is simple. Dictionaries are not infallible. They are made by humans and humans make mistakes. One person presented a misunderstanding of how the word was defined and this definition was repeated over and over again both orally and in print until it became a commonly accepted meaning for the word but just because something is *commonly accepted* does not mean that it is true. Something is only true, regardless of how many people believe it, when it is based upon what the evidence points towards being true. I believe that it has been ably demonstrated that the normal usage of *porneia* before, during and after the New Testament did not carry with it the idea of adultery and, as shown above, there are numerous dictionaries which do give the correct definition. Therefore, we must go with the evidence and rely on dictionaries that also go with the evidence, not with what some ill-prepared dictionaries may say.

Objection 7: If the Adultery View is not the correct interpretation then why did some of the great preachers from the past teach it?

The question could be asked, and rightfully so, that if the Adultery View is not correct why did some of the great preachers such as John Gill and Charles Spurgeon teach it. I believe that the answer to this question has to do with the fact that divorce was so *uncommon* in their day. Prior to 1857, when the British government loosened its strict divorce laws, there was only on average three divorces a year in England. That is right, that is not a "typo". Prior to the Matrimonial Causes Act of

---

[124] *A Compendious Dictionary Of The English Language* (New-Haven: Sidney's Press, 1806), Preface

1857 there was only an average of *three* divorces a year.[125] This was because in order to get a divorce (even in the case of adultery) an individual would normally have to:

1.) Raise the $82,000+ dollars that it would take to cover the divorce costs.[126]
2.) Go to the Ecclesiastical Court and there obtain against the adulterous spouse a decree of separation.
3.) Go to the secular courts and obtain a judgment against the spouse's adulterous partner.
4.) Go to Parliament and present this information with the hopes that they will pass an Act of Parliament granting the divorce (yes, you literally had to have an act of Congress in order to get a divorce granted).[127]

A similar story could be told for the United States. In the year 1867 for roughly every 100 marriages recorded, only *three divorces* were granted.[128] To give this a little perspective, in 2009 for every 100 marriages

---

[125] John Campbell (1779-1861) was the British politician who served as chairman of the committee whose report ultimately led to the passing of the new law to loosen Britain's strict divorce laws. In a letter dated January 10, 1859 (one year after the new law had went into effect) Campbell noted that prior to the change in the law, "Upon an average, I believe there were not in England above three divorces a year". (*Life Of John Lord Campbell, Vol. 2,* American Edition (Jersey City, NJ: Frederick D. Linn & Co., 1881), p.432).

[126] This was for a divorce under the most favorable of circumstances. If the case involved a large amount of litigation it could run into the hundreds of thousands of dollars. Frederick Clifford, *A History Of Private Bill Legislation, Vol. 1,* (London: Butterworths, 1885), p.422, footnote 2. Peter N. Stearns, *The Operation Of The 1857 Divorce Act, 1860-1910, A Research Note* in *The Journal Of Social History, Vol. 16, No. 4* (Summer 1983), pp.103-110. The increase for inflation reflected in the above amount was calculated using www.measuringworth.com.

[127] Henry Edwin Fenn, *Thirty-Five Years In The Divorce Court,* (Boston: Little, Brown & Co., 1911), pp.9-10.

[128] *100 Years Of Marriage And Divorce Statistics United States, 1867-1967,* Data From The National Vital Statistics System, Ser. 21, No. 24, DHEW Publication No. (HRA) 74-1902, (Health Resources Administration: U.S. Department Of Health, Education And Welfare, December, 1973), p.6.

entered into *50 divorces* were granted.[129] For statistical purposes this creates a dissolution rate of 3% in 1867 compared to 50% in 2009.

And a similar story could also be told for Canada. In the thirty four year period extending from 1867-1901 there were only 69 divorces in the whole country.[130]

The reason that some of the great preachers from the past did not question the Adultery View was because they really never had any reason to look into it. With divorces being pretty rare (in some cases as low as three a year) and the demand of more pressing pastoral duties there was never really much need to focus attention on the issue. Pastoral ministry can be an extremely time consuming vocation. If your job was to be a chef at a home for vegetarians you wouldn't spend your time studying how to cook meat and, similarly, you wouldn't spend your time studying who can divorce and remarry if no one in your parish was doing it. The great preachers from the past were just simply not faced with divorce and remarriage on the level that pastors today are and, therefore, never made it a matter of deep inquiry.

Connected closely with this is the fact that even though people have always gotten divorces where legal means allowed it, in the past there was such a stigma placed upon divorce that those who did obtain one would not normally go to church. In September of 1940, TIME Magazine ran an article on divorce and remarriage and the very first line of the article read, *"Fifty years ago few divorced persons were so brazen as to appear in any church."*[131] Divorce just was not an issue for some of the great preachers from the past. It was rare to begin with and even rarer to find a divorcee in the church. Logically, we would not expect the pastors of the past to have made it a matter of careful inquiry under these circumstances but instead to have just accepted what they had been taught while focusing their energy on more pressing issues.

---

[129] *Births, Marriages, Divorces, And Deaths: Provisional Data For 2009* in *National Vital Statistics Report, Vol. 58, No. 25* (U.S. Department Of Health And Human Services, Centers For Disease Control, August 27, 2010), p.1.

[130] W. S. Harwood, *The Divorce Situation In Canada* in *The World To-Day, Vol. 6, No. 2, February 1904* (Chicago: The World To-Day Co., 1904), p.193.

[131] "Religion: Episcopalians and Divorce" in TIME Magazine, Monday, Sep. 16, 1940.

Objection 8: Aren't there some post-New Testament Greek quotes which prove that *porneia* carried with it the idea of adultery?

There are two passages which have been given as evidence that *porneia*, at least in post-New Testament Greek literature, could be used to refer to adultery. We will look at these two passages by beginning with the most common one.

The most commonly cited passage comes from a 2nd century (c.160AD) document known as the *Shepherd Of Hermas*. It is a fictional account of a man's discussion with an angel about adultery and is as follows:

> And I said to him, "Sir, if any one has a wife who trusts in the Lord, and if he detect her in <u>adultery</u> (*moicheia*), does the man sin if he continue to live with her?" And he said to me, "As long as he remains ignorant of her sin, the husband commits no transgression in living with her. But if the husband know that his wife has gone astray, and if the woman does not repent, but persists in her <u>fornication</u> (*porneia*), and yet the husband continues to live with her, he also is guilty of her crime, and a sharer in her <u>adultery</u> (*moicheia*)." (*The Shepherd, Book 2, Commandment 4.1*)

After reading this passage I can see why some have looked at this and felt that Hermas was using *porneia* as if it was a synonym for *moicheia* (adultery). That would be the clear reading of the passage. The problem, however, is that scholars are not really sure if *porneia* is the word that Hermas originally used in this passage.

The reason for this is that the Greek of the *Shepherd Of Hermas* has not come down to us in a complete form. Instead, it has been pieced together from some twenty five different incomplete manuscripts that each contained a portion of the document. For some of it, the Greek has never been discovered, and for this scholars rely on ancient Latin translations to complete it.[132] The above passage, which is cited in numerous books advocating the Adultery View, is found in only two of

---

[132] Bart Ehrman, *The Apostolic Fathers, Vol. 2* (Cambridge, MA: Harvard University Press, 2003), p.169-171.

these manuscripts yet they disagree as to whether *porneia* should be in this passage or not.

The above translation comes from the Codex Sinaiticus which describes the adulterous wife as one who "persists in her <u>fornication</u> (*porneia*)". However, the other manuscript, the Codex Athos, leaves out the word *porneia* in this passage altogether, instead using the Greek word for "sin". The Athos version reads, "but persists in her <u>sin</u> (*hamartia*)".[133]

This passage is the main proof-text given from *all* of Greek literature as evidence that *porneia* carries with it the meaning of adultery. It is cited more often than any other supposed passage yet, as the above discrepancies show, it is far from being a solid, concrete piece of evidence. Kirsopp Lake is a respected scholar who has researched the underlying Greek text of the *Shepherd Of Hermas*. In 1913 he published a Greek text of the *Shepherd* which chose the Codex Sinaiticus reading over the Codex Athos' and this, undoubtedly, played a part in the popularity of advocates of the Adultery View using the *Shepherd* as a proof-text.[134] Yet, in his own preface he gives a word of warning to his readers to not place too much authority on the Greek text presented in his work:

"The text of Hermas [presented here] is probably far from good: the evidence of the papyri shows that <u>neither Codex Sinaiticus nor Codex Athos is completely trustworthy</u>, and it is unfortunate that for so large a part of the book Codex Athos is the only continuous Greek text."[135]

---

[133] Anyone with even a limited knowledge of Greek can confirm this discrepancy by comparing the Codex Sinaiticus (available at www.codexsinaiticus.org) with the Athos Codex whose photographs and transcription were published in Kirsopp Lake's *Facsimiles Of The Athos Fragments Of The Shepherd Of Hermas* (Oxford: Clarendon Press, 1907). Note that www.codexsinaiticus.org uses the new numbering system for *The Shepherd* and under this system the passage in question is 29:5.

[134] Strangely, and perhaps worth noting here, Lake's edition changed the spelling of *porneia* from the way that it was spelled in Codex Sinaiticus. Sinaiticus has is spelled *pornia*.

[135] *The Apostolic Fathers With An English Translation, Vol. 2*, (London: William Heinemann, 1913, 1917 reprint), p.5.

So, even a *Shepherd Of Hermas* scholar is telling people to not rely too heavily upon the Greek text of this passage.

When one looks at the *Shepherd of Hermas* as a whole, they will see that it makes a lot more sense for that word to be *hamartia* (the Greek word for sin) than it does for it to be *porneia*.

First, Hermas indicated in another passage that he understood *porneia* and adultery to be two different things:

> "What, sir," say I, "are the evil deeds from which we must restrain ourselves?" "Hear," says he: "from **adultery** (*moicheia*) and **fornication** (*porneia*), from unlawful reveling, from wicked luxury, from indulgence in many kinds of food and the extravagance of riches..." (*The Shepherd, Book 2, Commandment 8:3/Kirsopp Lake*[136])

Secondly, Hermas himself, in the very passage as it is presented by advocates of the Adultery View, rejects the idea that adultery enables a husband to divorce and remarry:

> **'But if the husband know that his wife has gone astray, and if the woman does not repent, but persists in her fornication, and yet the husband continues to live with her, he also is guilty of her crime, and a sharer in her adultery.' And I said to him, 'What then, sir, is the husband to do, if his wife continue in her vicious practices?' And he said, 'The husband should put her away, and remain by himself. <u>But if he put his wife away and marry another, he also commits adultery</u>.'**

One would assume that Hermas had read the Gospel of Matthew and was, therefore, familiar with its exception clause for *porneia*. If Hermas had understood the word *porneia* to carry with it the idea of adultery and had actually used it in this passage to refer to adultery, then it would only make sense that he would have interpreted the exception clause to mean that adultery would allow a man to divorce and remarry. Yet, in this passage, the man whose wife has committed adultery is told

---

[136] Greek text from Kirsopp Lake's *The Apostolic Fathers With An English Translation, Vol. 2: The Shepherd Of Hermas, The Martyrdom Of Polycarp, & The Epistle To Diognetus* (London: William Heinemann, 1917), p. 102.

that if he does put his wife away and marry someone else, then he is also committing a sin.

All this shows us that *hamartia* is more likely the correct word for this passage and that using *porneia* here causes Hermas to contradict himself in at least two ways.[137]

As I mentioned this is the most cited evidence presented in favor of the Adultery View but it is far from solid evidence. At the best, it is a weak argument and it would be very unwise to base a decision that could send a person to hell for all eternity upon a manuscript that a *Shepherd* scholar has warned against being trustworthy and for which there is an alternate reading which falls in line with the historical and linguistical data presented above.

But, let's say for the sake of argument that *porneia* is the correct word in this passage—*would that mean that the exception clause was referring to adultery?* Not necessarily. Remember that one of the ancient uses for *porneia* was "prostitution" because this was a profession entered into by primarily *single people having pre-marital sex* and that occasionally this word was used to refer to married women who became prostitutes. Two parts of the *Shepherd* would imply that in this passage Hermas was not referring to adultery (if indeed he had actually used the word *porneia* here). The first is that Hermas did not use the word *porneia* to refer to adultery as noted in his distinction between adultery and *porneia* in Book 2, Commandment 8:3 mentioned above and the second is the behavior of the adulterous wife. In the passage Hermas asks the angel, *"What then, sir, is the husband to do, if his wife continue in her vicious practices?"* The angel

---

[137] It would probably be appropriate to note here that there are people today who believe that the Codex Sinaiticus is a 19th century forgery, not a 4th century original. In 1862, Dr. Constantine Simonides, a known manuscript forger, claimed to have created a manuscript of the Bible and Apostolic Fathers made to look like an ancient copy complete with ancient lettering on aged parchment that had been intended as a gift for Emperor Nicholas I of Russia. The gift was never finished, according to Simonides, and eventually ended up in Saint Catherine's Monastery where it was "discovered" and assumed to have been a real ancient copy. Others, rejecting Simonides claim, have questioned the truthfulness of Constantin von Tischendorf (the discoverer of the manuscript) and how he claims to have found it. Simonides' claim to creating it himself was published in *The Journal Of Sacred Literature And Biblical Record, No. 3, October 1862* in *Vol 2: New Series* (Edinburgh: Williams & Norgate, 1863) p.248-250.

responds that *"The husband should put her away"*. I don't think that the man would have to put her away if she had fell into an adulterous love affair as she most likely would run off with her lover. But this is a woman who is 1.) Having sex outside of marriage; 2.) Seems to have no intention of leaving (the angel tells the husband that he would need to initiate putting her away); and 3.) Is engaging in a behavior which is described by a Greek word that lexicons acknowledge can mean prostitution. If there was not an alternate reading for this passage which made more sense then I would assume, based upon the normal usage of *porneia* in Greek literature and the evidence within the *Shepherd* that this passage seems more descriptive of a married woman who has become secretly involved in prostitution for financial gain and is discovered by her husband than a woman who has become involved in an intimate and personal adulterous relationship.

And this brings us to another passage that has been suggested as indicating that *porneia* in post-New Testament Greek literature carried with it the idea of adultery.

This passage is from a document believed to have been completed around the year 192AD which is known as the *Testament Of The Twelve Patriarchs*. It is a fictitious account of the lives of the twelve children of Jacob but before we look at it we need to examine a little more about the ancient relationship between prostitution and slavery.

Many Greek scholars are persuaded that the root of *porneia* (*porne*) comes from *pernemi* which means "to sell" and this connection is believed to have existed because Greek prostitutes were usually slaves. This is confirmed by *The Theological Dictionary Of The New Testament*,[138] *Vine's Complete Expository Dictionary of Old and New Testament Words*,[139] *The Oxford Classical Dictionary*,[140] and *The New American Standard Exhaustive*

---

[138] "*porne* (from *pernemi*, 'to sell') literally means 'harlot for hire' (Greek harlots were usually slaves)." Geoffrey William Bromiley, *Vol. 1*, (Grand Rapids, MI: William B. Eerdmans Publishing, 1985), p.918.

[139] "*porne* ($\pi\acute{o}\rho\nu\eta$, 4204) 'a prostitute, harlot' (from *pernemi*, 'to sell')..." W. E. Vine (Thomas Nelson Publishers, 1996), p. 291, entry for "Harlot".

[140] "The very terms *porneion* (brothel) and *porne* (whore) are related to *pernemi* (to sell)..." Simon Hornblower & Antony Spawforth (Oxford University Press, USA, 1996), p. 1264, entry for "prostitution, secular".

Concordance of the Bible: Hebrew-Aramaic and Greek Dictionaries.[141] Lexicons seem pretty much in agreement that the stem of *porneia* (*porne*) by itself means prostitute and sometimes *porneia* is used to describe prostitution.

With this in mind, it should not surprise us to read in Greek literature about the sexual behavior of bought and sold slaves as being that of *porneia*. And that brings us to our second passage that has been cited in favor of *porneia* meaning adultery. That passage is the *Testament Of The Twelve Patriarchs'* description of Joseph's temptation to commit a sexual sin with the wife of Potiphar.

> "These my brethren hated me, and the Lord loved me: they wished to slay me, and the God of my fathers guarded me: they let me down into a pit, and the Most High brought me up again: I was **sold for a slave**...I was taken into captivity, and His strong hand succored me: And thus Potiphar the chief cook of Pharaoh entrusted to me his house, and I struggled against a shameless woman, urging me to transgress with her...Last of all, she sought to **draw me into *porneia***."[142]

Many have pointed to this passage as evidence that *porneia* means adultery, for here you have a married woman trying to draw a man other than her husband into adultery and this situation is described as *porneia*. On the surface, I would agree that this appears to be good evidence that *porneia* can be used to describe adulterous behavior. However, I believe that if we look at the whole picture what we will see is that Joseph's temptation to sexual sin is being described as *porneia* because he is a "slave" and as such he is not saying, "Last of all, she sought to draw me into adultery" but rather "she sought to draw me into *prostitution*." And there are good reasons for assuming this. First, it does not violate the normal usage of the Greek word *porneia* for it to be interpreted here as referring to prostitution. Indeed, the fact that Joseph was a slave would have qualified that word to be used about him in this situation in this manner. Secondly, the author of the *Testament Of The Twelve Patriarchs*

---

[141] "4204. πόρνη porne; prob. from pernemi πέρνεμι (*to export for sale*)..." (Foundation Publications, 1998), p. 1559.

[142] *The Testament Of Joseph, 11:1-3.* The underlying Greek text is from PG 2:1128.

elsewhere demonstrates that he did not believe that adultery and *porneia* were the same thing:

> "Another committeth **adultery** (*moicheuo*) and **fornication** (*porneuo*), and abstaineth from meats; yet in his fasting he worketh evil, and by his power and his wealth perverteth many..." (*10:2, The Testimony Of Asher, Sec. 2/ PG 2:1121*)

Numerous examples have been given to show that *porneia* is something different than adultery (including this one from the very document that we are discussing). It only makes sense to interpret *The Testaments'* usage of *porneia* in such a way that it matches with Greek literature's normal usage of the word (including how the very document itself uses it). And that evidence would suggest here that the issue was prostitution, not adultery.

But, again, let's say for the sake of argument, that one did find a piece of Greek literature written centuries after the time of Jesus which did use *porneia* in an unusual and out of the ordinary manner to describe adultery. Would that mean that the "exception clause" was definitely talking about adultery? No. It would only mean that a Greek writer, many years after Matthew's Gospel was written, had used a word in an abnormal way contrary to the way in which Greek writers normally used that same word. An individual could write their own book using the word "elephant" in an unusual way to describe a dog but that does not mean that the word "elephant" is always going to be referring to a dog in all of the literature written before the book on elephants.

Even if a word could be found being used over a century and a half *after* the time of Jesus in an unusual way that would only prove that the word at that time was being used in that way, not that it was used in Jesus' day in that way. To give a practical illustration for this no one would seriously suggest using a 20th century newspaper article to define the vocabulary of a 16th century book. Why then, do individuals suggest using Greek literature, perhaps written centuries after the New Testament to define its vocabulary? That does not make very much sense.

The Adultery View Has Been
Rejected By Christians Throughout History

It may surprise many Christians today who have never heard of an alternative view but there have *always* been Christian men and women who rejected the Adultery View. In my research I was able to find individuals from *every century* since the time of Jesus and this is what I would like to offer as the final reason that led me to reject the Adultery View in favor of the Fornication View. I think that it is interesting, and worth noting, that some of these people did believe that *porneia* in Matthew's exception clause was referring to adultery, yet they still did not understand the passage to allow remarriage after a divorce.[143] The student of God's Word who finds himself having doubts about the validity of the Adultery View can be assured that he is surrounded by millions of Christians who have shared his doubts.

Justin Martyr (c.100-165AD)

And, "Whoever shall marry her that is divorced from another husband, commits adultery." And, "There are some who have been made eunuchs of men, and some who were born eunuchs, and some who have made themselves eunuchs for the kingdom of heaven's sake; but all cannot receive this saying." So that **all who, by human law, are twice married, are in the eye of our Master sinners**, and those who look upon a woman to lust after her.[144]

Hermas (fl. c.160AD)

And I said to him, "Sir, if any one has a wife who trusts in the Lord, and if he detect her in adultery, does the man sin if he continues to live with her?" And he said to me, "As long as he remains ignorant of her sin, the

---

[143] In some cases I have modernized the older English of some of these translations of Latin and Greek documents. These have been marked with an "*" in their respective footnotes followed by the original source of the quote. In some cases where it seemed clear that the original author was using the Latin *fornicatio* or one of its variants to refer to adultery this was rendered as "immorality", although this word in Latin seems to usually refer to premarital sex or prostitution. Quotations originally written in English, however, have been left unaltered.

[144] *The First Apology, 15.** Alexander Roberts, James Donaldson, & A. Cleveland Coxe, *The Ante-Nicene Fathers: The Writings Of The Fathers Down To A.D. 325, Vol. 1* in *The Master Christian Library CD-ROM, 8.0* (Albany, OR: Ages, 1997). Hereafter referred to as ANF.

husband commits no transgression in living with her. But if the husband knows that his wife has gone astray, and if the woman does not repent, but persists in her sin, and yet the husband continues to live with her, he also is guilty of her crime, and a sharer in her adultery." And I said to him, "What then, sir, is the husband to do, if his wife continues in her vicious practices?" And he said, "The husband should put her away, **and remain by himself. But if he put his wife away and marry another, he also commits adultery**."[145]

Theophilus (fl. c. 170-190AD)

"And he that marries," says [the Gospel], "her that is divorced from her husband, commits adultery; and whoever puts away his wife, saving for the cause of fornication, causes her to commit adultery." Because Solomon says: "Can a man take fire in his bosom, and his clothes not be burned? Or can one walk upon hot coals, and his feet not be burned? **So he that goes in to a married woman shall not be innocent**."[146]

Athenagoras (fl. c. 177AD)

For we bestow our attention; not on the study of words, but on the exhibition and teaching of actions, — that a person should either remain as he was born, or **be content with one marriage**; for a second marriage is only a specious adultery. "For whoever puts away his wife," says He, "and marries another, commits adultery;" **not permitting a man to send her away whose virginity he has brought to an end,[147] nor to marry again**.[148]

Clement Of Alexandria (d. c. 215AD)

Now that the Scripture counsels marriage, and allows **no release from the union**, is expressly contained in the law, "You shall not put away your wife, except for the cause of fornication;" and **it regards as adultery the marriage of those separated while the other is alive**[149]…The Church

---

[145] *The Shepherd, Second Book, Commandment 4:1,** ANF, Vol. 2. Amended according to Codex Athos.

[146] *To Autolycus, 3:13,** ANF, Vol. 2.

[147] This appears to be a reference to the Fornication View.

[148] *A Plea For The Christians, 33,** ANF, Vol. 2.

[149] *The Stromata, 2:23,** ANF, Vol. 2. I have corrected a translation error here according to PG 9:1096.

cannot marry another, having obtained a bridegroom; but each of us individually has the right to marry the woman he wishes according to the law; I mean here **first marriage**.[150]

Tertullian (c.160-c.220AD)

A divorced woman cannot even marry legitimately; and if she commits any such act without the name of marriage, does it not fall under the category of adultery, in that adultery is crime in the way of marriage? Such is God's verdict, within narrower limits than men's, that universally, whether through marriage or promiscuously, the admission of a second man to intercourse is pronounced adultery by Him...So true, moreover, is it that divorce "was not from the beginning," that among the Romans it is not till after the six hundredth year from the building of the city that this kind of "hard-heartedness" is set down as having been committed. But they indulge in promiscuous adulteries, even without divorcing their partners: to us, **even if we do divorce them, even marriage will not be lawful**.[151]

Council Of Arles (314AD)

Of those who discover their wives in adultery and are young Christians and are forbidden to marry, it was determined that they be most strongly advised **not to take other wives while their own live, though they be adulterous**.[152]

Council Of Elvira (324AD)

A Christian woman who has left an adulterous Christian husband and is marrying another is to be forbidden to marry; if, however, she has already remarried, she is not to receive communion before the death of the man whom she has left, unless mortal sickness compels it.[153]

---

[150] *The Stromata, 3:11:74*. Henry Chadwick & John Ernest Leonard Oulton, *The Library of Christian Classics: Volume II, Alexandrian Christianity: Selected Translations of Clement and Origen* (Philadelphia, PA: Westminster Press, 1954).

[151] *On Monogamy, 9*,* ANF Vol. 4.

[152] *Canon 10*. Cited in *"Divorce"* in *The Church Quarterly Review, Vol. XL, No. LXXIX, April 1895* (London: Spottiswoode & Co, 1895), p.21.

[153] *Canon 9*. See also this passage in *"Divorce"* in *The Church Quarterly Review, Vol. XL, No. LXXIX, April 1895* (London: Spottiswoode & Co, 1895), p.21.

Gregory Nazianzen (c.325-389AD)

For I think that the Word here seems to deprecate second marriage. For, if there were two Christs, there may be two husbands or two wives; but if Christ is One, one Head of the Church, let there be also one flesh, and let a second be rejected...Now the Law grants divorce for every cause; but Christ not for every cause; but He allows **only separation** from the whore; and in all other things He commands patience.[154]

Ambrose Of Milan (333-397AD)

Therefore, the right to marry is given to you, lest ye fall into a snare and sin with a strange woman. Ye are bound to your wife; do not seek release because **you are not permitted to marry another while your wife lives**.[155]

John Chrysostom (c.347-407AD)

'Let her remain unmarried or be reconciled to her husband.'....'What then if he will never be reconciled?' one may ask. You have one more mode of release and deliverance. *What is that?* Await his death. For as the (consecrated) virgin may not marry because her Spouse always lives, and is immortal; so to her who has been married it is then **only lawful** [to remarry] when her husband is dead.[156]

Apostolic Canons (c.400AD)[157]

If a layman divorces his own wife, and takes another, or one divorced by another, let him be suspended.[158]

Council Of Mileve (416AD)[159]

---

[154] *Oration 37:8.* Philip Schaff, *The Nicene And Post Nicene Fathers, Series 2, Vol. 7* (Albany, OR: Ages, 1997). Hereafter referred to as NPNF.

[155] *On Abraham The Patriarch, 1:7:59.* Theodosia Tomkinson, Tr. (Etba, CA: Center For Traditionalist Orthodox Studies, 2000)

[156] *On Virginity, 40.** Cited in Oscar Daniel Watkins, *Holy Matrimony* (London: Rivington, Percival & Co., 1895), p.311-12.

[157] This canon laid down the rule that any layperson that divorced and remarried (under any circumstances) was to be suspended (excommunicated) from the church.

[158] *Canon 48.* In some collections this may be numbered 47. ANF, Vol. 7.

[159] This canon forbid persons who had been abandoned by their spouses from remarrying. Surely, in some case of abandonment adultery either did or would

According to the evangelical and apostolic discipline it is decreed that neither a man who is put away by his wife, nor a woman put away by her husband, may marry another, but that they must either abide so, or be reconciled to each other.[160]

Innocent I (d. 417AD)

It is manifest that **when persons who have been divorced marry again both parties are adulterers**. And moreover, although the former marriage is supposed to be broken, yet if they marry again they themselves are adulterers, but the parties whom they marry are equally with them guilty of adultery; as we read in the gospel: *He who puts away his wife and marries another commits adultery;* and likewise, *He who marries her that is put away from her husband commits adultery.* Therefore all such are to be repelled from communion.[161]

Council Of Carthage (a.k.a. African Code, 419AD)[162]

It was determined that, in accordance with Evangelical and Apostolic discipline, neither a man put away by his wife nor a woman put away by her husband may be united to another; but let them remain so, or be reconciled to each other.[163]

Jerome (c.340-420AD)

The apostle has thus cut away every plea and has clearly declared that, **if a woman marries again while her husband is living, she is an adulteress**. You must not speak to me of the violence of a ravisher, a mother's pleading, a father's bidding, the influence of relatives, the insolence and the intrigues of servants, household losses. **A husband may be an adulterer** or a sodomite, he may be stained with every crime and

---

occur yet the above decree forbids *in every case* the remarriage of the abandoned partners.

[160] *Canon 17.* Cited in John Fulton *The Laws Of Marriage* (New York, NY: E. & J. B. Young, 1883), p.255.

[161] *Letter To Exsuperius, Bishop of Toulouse, Ch.6.** Cited in John Fulton *The Laws Of Marriage* (New York, NY: E. & J. B. Young, 1883), p.255.

[162] This one is a recapitulation of the above decree of the Council of Mileve which forbade abandoned spouses to remarry.

[163] *Canon 102.* Cited in *"Divorce"* in *The Church Quarterly Review, Vol. XL, No. LXXIX, April 1895* (London: Spottiswoode & Co, 1895), p.22.

may have been left by his wife because of his sins; **yet he is still her husband and, so long as he lives, she may not marry another**.[164]

Augustine Of Hippo (354-430AD)

It cannot be correctly affirmed either that the husband who puts away his wife because of immorality and marries another does not commit adultery. **For there is adultery, also, on the part of those who marry others after the repudiation of their former wives because of immorality**...If everyone who marries another woman after the dismissal of his wife commits adultery, this includes the one who puts away his wife without the cause of immorality **and the one who puts away his wife for this reason**.[165]

Council Of Angers (453AD)[166]

They who abuse the name of marriage by taking women [as their wives] whose husbands are living shall be excommunicated.[167]

Finnian (a.k.a. Vinnian, Vinnianus, Finian, d.c.550AD)

If a man's wife commits immorality and cohabits with another man, he ought not to take another wife while his wife is alive.[168]

Adamnan (c.624-704AD)

Of a wife who is a harlot, thus the same man explained, "That she will be a harlot, who has cast off the yoke of her own husband, and is joined to a

---

[164] *Letter 55:3, To Amandus*. NPNF, Series 2, Vol. 6.

[165] *Adulterous Marriage, 1:9*. Roy Joseph Deferrari & Charles T. Wilcox, *Fathers Of The Church, Vol. 27: Treatises On Marriage And Other Subjects* (Washington, DC: CUA Press, 1999).

[166] This appears to be a complete prohibition against divorced women remarrying, even in the case of adultery.

[167] *Canon 6*. Cited in John Fulton *The Laws Of Marriage* (New York, NY: E. & J. B. Young, 1883), p.255.

[168] *Penitential of Vinnian, Sec. 43.** John Thomas McNeill & Helena Margaret Gamer, *Medieval Handbooks Of Penance: A Translation Of The Principal "Libri Poenitentiales" And Selections From Related Documents* (New York, NY: Columbia University Press, 1938, 1990), p.95.

second or a third husband; and her husband shall not take another [wife] while she lives…"[169]

Council Of Nantes (658AD)

If a man's wife has committed adultery…let him send away his wife, if he will…But her husband may not on any account take another wife while she lives.[170]

Council Of Hertford (673AD)

Concerning Marriage: That none but lawful matrimony be allowed to any; That no man contract an incestuous marriage; That none quit his own wife, except (as the holy Gospel teaches) on account of fornication; That **supposing any to have expelled his own wife united to him in lawful matrimony, if he choose to be a Christian indeed, he must connect himself with no other woman, but must so abide**, or be reconciled to his own wife.[171]

Judicium Clementis (693AD)[172]

If any man sends away his lawful wife and marries another, he is to be excommunicated by Christians, even if the first wife consent…It is not lawful for separation to take place in the case of a lawful marriage unless there is the consent of both, **so that they may remain unmarried**.[173]

Venerable Bede (c.672-735AD)

---

[169] *Canons Of Adamnan, Canon 16,* John Thomas McNeill & Helena Margaret Gamer, *Medieval Handbooks Of Penance: A Translation Of The Principal "Libri Poenitentiales" And Selections From Related Documents* (New York, NY: Columbia University Press, 1965), p.133.

[170] *Canon 12.* Cited in *"Divorce"* in *The Church Quarterly Review, Vol. XL, No. LXXIX, April 1895* (London: Spottiswoode & Co, 1895), p.18.

[171] *Canon 10.* Cited in John Keble *Sequel Of The Argument Against Immediately Repealing The Laws Which Treat The Nuptial Bond As Indissoluble* (London: J.H. & Jas. Parker, 1857), p.197-198.

[172] This document was an Anglo-Saxon manual on penance and it gives us an idea of what the 7th century Anglo-Saxon Christians believed regarding divorce and remarriage.

[173] *Sec. 14-15.** Cited in *"Divorce"* in *The Church Quarterly Review, Vol. XL, No. LXXIX, April 1895* (London: Spottiswoode & Co, 1895), p.8.

Therefore is there only one carnal cause, fornication: one spiritual cause, the fear of God for which a wife may be dismissed. But **there is no cause prescribed by the law of God that another wife may be taken, while she is alive who has been abandoned**.[174]

Council Of Trullo (692AD)[175]

She who has left her husband is an adulteress if she has come to another, according to the holy and divine Basil, who has gathered this most excellently from the prophet Jeremiah…he who leaves the wife lawfully given him, and shall take another is guilty of adultery by the sentence of the Lord.[176]

Council Of Soissons (744AD)[177]

We ordain that…no one take the wife of another while her husband is living, and that no woman take another husband while her own is living; because a husband ought not to send away his wife except for the cause of discovered fornication.[178]

Zacharias (d. 752AD)

Concerning a layman repelling his wife from the canon of the holy apostles, chapter 48: **If any layman repelling his own wife has taken another or one dismissed by another, let him be deprived of Communion**[179]…Concerning those who dismiss their wives or husbands, that they remain thus: from the African Council above mentioned in chapter 69 it is thus contained: it was resolved that according to

---

[174] *On The Gospel Of Mark, Ch. 10.* Cited in Henry John Wilkins *The History Of Divorce And Re-marriage For English Churchmen* (London: Longmans, Green & Co., 1910), p.124.

[175] This canon appears to be a complete prohibition against putting away one's spouse and remarrying, even in the case of adultery.

[176] *Canon 87.* NPNF, Series 2, Vol. 14.

[177] This appears to be a prohibition against marrying a person who has been divorced under any circumstances while their first spouse is still alive, even if they were an adulterer.

[178] *Canon 9.* Cited in *"Divorce"* in *The Church Quarterly Review, Vol. XL, No. LXXIX, April 1895* (London: Spottiswoode & Co, 1895), p.16.

[179] This prohibition against a layperson putting away his wife and marrying another included those who put their wives away for adultery.

evangelical and apostolical discipline, neither a man dismissed by his wife, nor a woman dismissed by her husband, may be joined to another; but that they so remain or be mutually reconciled.[180]

Excerptions Of Egbert (d.766AD)

Augustine says, 'If a woman commits immorality she is to be dismissed; **but another is not to be married while she is alive**.' Wherever, then, there is immorality, and a just suspicion of immorality, the wife may be freely dismissed…According to the Evangelical discipline, neither let a wife, dismissed from her husband, take another man, the former living; nor a husband another woman; but let them so remain, or be reconciled. Augustine says: 'If a woman commits immorality she is to be relinquished, **but another must not be taken so long as she lives**.'[181]

Synod Of Aachen (789AD)

Also it was decreed in the same (African Council) that neither a wife, dismissed by a husband, may take another husband, while her own husband is alive, nor a husband take another wife, while his first wife still lives.[182]

Council Of Friuli (791AD)

Though the bond of marriage be broken for the cause of immorality, a man may not marry another wife as long as the adulteress lives, though she be an adulteress; and the adulteress shall never marry another husband.[183]

Sixth Council Of Paris (829AD)

---

[180] *Letter 7 To Pippin, Ch.7, 12.** Cited in Henry John Wilkins *The History Of Divorce And Re-marriage For English Churchmen* (London: Longmans, Green & Co., 1910), p.99-100.

[181] *Canons 119-121.** Cited in *"Divorce"* in *The Church Quarterly Review, Vol. XL, No. LXXIX, April 1895* (London: Spottiswoode & Co, 1895), p.11.

[182] *Canon 13.* Cited in Henry John Wilkins *The History Of Divorce And Re-marriage For English Churchmen* (London: Longmans, Green & Co., 1910), p.108.

[183] *Canon 10.** Cited in *"Divorce"* in *The Church Quarterly Review, Vol. XL, No. LXXIX, April 1895* (London: Spottiswoode & Co, 1895), p.17 & John Fulton *The Laws Of Marriage* (New York, NY: E. & J. B. Young, 1883), p.258-9.

And those who marry other wives when their own have been sent away for the cause of immorality are to be marked as adulterers by the judgment of the Lord.[184]

Canon List Of Benedict the Levite (c.847AD)

That during the lifetime of husband or wife neither of them be united in another marriage...And **if she has committed immorality, and her husband desires it, she is to be dismissed, but another wife may not be taken in marriage during her lifetime**, because adulterers will not possess the kingdom of God, and her penitence is to be accepted.[185]

Laws of the Northumbrian Priests (950AD)[186]

If any man dismiss his lawful wife [while she is] living and marry another, let him want God's mercy unless he make satisfaction for it; but let every one retain his lawful wife so long as she lives, unless they both choose to be separated by the bishop's consent and are willing to preserve their chastity for the future.[187]

The Penitential Of Archbishop Dunston (c. 963AD)

He that relinquishes his wife [for any reason] and takes another woman breaks wedlock. Let none of those rights which belong to Christians be allowed him, either during life, or at his death, nor let him be buried with Christian men: and let the same be done to a [delinquent] wife: and let the kindred that were present at the contract [of the second marriage] suffer

---

[184] *Canon 2.* Cited in *"Divorce"* in *The Church Quarterly Review, Vol. XL, No. LXXIX, April 1895* (London: Spottiswoode & Co, 1895), p.18.

[185] Joseph Friesen, *Geschichte Des Canonischen Eherechts* (Zweigniederlassungen: Druck Und Verlag Von Ferdinand Schöningh, 1893), p.793. Cited in Oscar Daniel Watkins, *Holy Matrimony* (London: Rivington, Percival & Co., 1895), p.391.*

[186] The following law indicated that if a separation did take place under any circumstances the two spouses had to live chastely for the rest of their lives which would have precluded any option of remarrying while both spouses still lived.

[187] *Section 54.* John Johnson, *A Collection Of the Laws And Canons Of The Church of England, Vol. 1* (Oxford: John Henry Parker, 1850), p.381.

the same doom, except they will first be converted, and earnestly make satisfaction.[188]

Council of Eanham (1009AD)

And let it never be, that a Christian man marry within the relationship of 6th persons, in his own kin, that is within the fourth degree; nor with the relict of him who was so near in worldly relationship; nor with the wife's relation, whom he before had had. Nor with any hallowed nun, nor with his god-mother, **nor with one divorced, let any Christian man ever marry**;[189] **nor have more wives than one, but be with that one, as long as she may live**; whoever will rightly observe God's law, and secure his soul from the burning of hell.[190]

Ecclesiastical Laws of King Cnut
(a.k.a. Canute, Knud, c.994-1035AD)

We enjoin, and charge, and command, in God's name, that no Christian man do ever take a wife of his own kin within the sixth degree of relation, nor the widow of a kinsman so nearly related to him, nor of the kindred of a wife whom he formerly had, nor of his sureties at baptism, nor a consecrated nun, **nor a divorced woman**, nor practice any unlawful copulation. **Let no man have more than one wife, and let her be a wedded wife, and let him remain with her only, so long as she lives**, if he will rightly observe God's will, and secure his soul against hell flames.[191]

Council Of Rheims (1049AD)

---

[188] *Sec. 27.* Cited in Henry John Wilkins *The History Of Divorce And Re-marriage For English Churchmen* (London: Longmans, Green & Co., 1910), p.124.

[189] This prohibited a man from marrying any woman who had been divorced, regardless of the cause (even adultery) and was therefore a rejection of the Adultery View.

[190] *The Laws Of King Ethelred (c. 968-1016), 6:12.* John Milton Stearns, *The Germs And Developments Of The Laws Of England* (New York, NY: Banks & Brothers, Law Publishers, 1889), p.175.

[191] *Ecclesiastical Laws of King Cnut, Law No. 7.* John Johnson, *A Collection Of the Laws And Canons Of The Church of England, Vol. 1* (Oxford: John Henry Parker, 1850), p.506.

[We decree] That no one, having left his lawful wife, may take another.[192]

John Gratian (d.1160)

If either the husband has departed from his wife, or the wife from the husband on the ground of immorality, it is unlawful to take another.[193]

Peter Lombard (c.1100-c.1164)

The marriage bond still exists between those who, even if departing from one another, having joined themselves to others.[194]

Alexander III (d.1181AD)

Marriage is dissolved by the adultery of the wife, but in such wise that neither party may marry again; and if the husband marry another woman, his second marriage is null, and the first marriage, with all its duties and obligations, is restored.[195]

Thomas Aquinas (c.1225-1274)

Nothing happening after a marriage can dissolve it: wherefore adultery does not make a marriage cease to be valid. For, according to Augustine (De Nup. et Concup. i, 10), "as long as they live they are bound by the marriage tie, which neither divorce nor union with another can destroy." Therefore it is unlawful for one, while the other lives, to marry again.[196]

John Wycliffe (1328-1384)

And let each man be aware that he procures no false divorce, for money, neither for friendship, neither for enemy; for Christ commands that no man separate them that God has joined; but only for adultery that party

---

[192] *Canon 12.* Cited in Henry John Wilkins *The History Of Divorce And Re-marriage For English Churchmen* (London: Longmans, Green & Co., 1910), p.109.

[193] *Decretum, Case 32, Question 7, C. 3.* Cited in Henry John Wilkins *The History Of Divorce And Re-marriage For English Churchmen* (London: Longmans, Green & Co., 1910), p.110.

[194] Cited in Henry John Wilkins *The History Of Divorce And Re-marriage For English Churchmen* (London: Longmans, Green & Co., 1910), p.111.

[195] *Decretals Of Gregory IX, 4.19.5.* Cited in John Fulton *The Laws Of Marriage* (New York, NY: E. & J. B. Young, 1883), p.260-261.

[196] *Summa Theologica, Part 3, Supplement, 62:5* (New York: Benziger Brothers, 1922), p.303.

that keeps himself clean may depart from the other's bed and for no other cause, as Christ himself says. And in this case the clean party has [only] **the option to either live chastely for as long as the other [spouse] lives, or else be reconciled again to the other party**.[197]

Council Of Florence (1431-1445)

A triple good is found in matrimony. The first is the begetting of children and their education to the worship of God. The second is the faithfulness which each spouse owes to the other. Third is the indissolubility of marriage, inasmuch as it represents the indissoluble union of Christ and the Church. But, **although it is permitted to separate on account of adultery, nevertheless it is not permitted to contract another marriage** since the bond of a marriage legitimately contracted is perpetual.[198]

A Necessary Doctrine And
Erudition For Any Christian Man (1543)[199]

Notwithstanding, in marriages lawfully made, and according to the ordinance of matrimony prescribed by God and the laws of every realm, **the bond thereof cannot be dissolved during the lives of the parties** between whom such matrimony is made.[200]

The Institution Of A Christian Man (1545)[201]

---

[197] *Of Weddid Men And Wifis And Of Here Children Also, Ch.2*, in Thomas Arnold, ed. *Select English Works Of John Wycliffe, Vol. 3: Miscellaneous Works* (Oxford: Clarendon Press, 1871), p.192.

[198] *Session 8—22 November 1439, [Bull of union with the Armenians]*. Cited in Herbert Vorgrimler *Sacramental Theology* (Collegeville, MN: Liturgical Press, 1992), p.296.

[199] This was an official document produced by the Anglican Church whose purpose was to give the English people everything that was "necessary" in order for them to understand the Christian life.

[200] *The Sacrament Of Matrimony*, in Charles Lloyd's *Formularies Of Faith Put Forth By Authority During The Reign Of Henry VIII* (Oxford: University Press, 1856), p.276-277.

[201] This was another official document produced by the Anglican Church to instruct the English people. As such, it shows us how the English in the 16th century viewed the issue of divorce and remarriage.

Notwithstanding in marriages lawfully made, and according to the ordinance of matrimony prescribed by God and holy church, **the bond thereof can by no means be dissolved during the lives of the parties** between whom such matrimony is contracted. [202]

Anglican Canons (1603)[203]

In all Sentences for Divorce, Bond to be taken for not marrying during each other's Life. In all sentences pronounced only for divorce and separation *a thoro et mensa*,[204] there shall be a caution and restraint inserted in the act of the said sentence, That the parties so separated shall live chastely and continently; neither shall they, during each other's life, contract matrimony with any other person. And, for the better observation of this last clause, the said sentence of divorce shall not be pronounced, until the party or parties requiring the same have given good and sufficient caution and security into the court, that they will not any way break or transgress the said restraint or prohibition. [205]

Lancelot Andrewes (1555-1626)

First, I take **the act of adultery doth not dissolve the bond of marriage**; for then it would follow, that the party offending would not, upon reconciliation, be received again by the innocent to former society of life, without a new solemnizing of marriage, insomuch as the former marriage is quite dissolved, which is never heard of, and contrary to the practice of all Churches... in my opinion, **second marriages (where either party is living) are not warranted by the word of God**.[206]

---

[202] *Part 2, Matrimony.* Charles Lloyd, *Formularies Of Faith Put Forth By Authority During The Reign Of Henry VIII* (Oxford: University Press, 1856), p.91-92.

[203] The Anglican Canons of 1603 were the official rules of practice for the Anglican Church.

[204] Divorce *a thoro et mensa* as it was understood by the 17th century English people will explained below in the quote from "Institutes of The Laws Of England".

[205] *Canon 107.* Edward Cardwell's *Synodalia: A Collection Of Articles Of Religion, Canons, And Proceedings Of Convocations In The Province of Canterbury, From The Year 1547 To The Year 1717, Vol. 1* (Oxford: University Press, 1842), p.307-308.

[206] *Against Second Marriage, After Sentence Of Divorce With A Former Match, The Party Then Living* in *Works: Two answers To Cardinal Perron And Other*

Institutes Of The Laws Of England
(First Published In Four Parts, 1628-1644)[207]

There be two kinds of divorces, the one that dissolveth the marriage *a vinculo matrimonii*;[208] as for precontract, consanguinity, &c. and the other *a mensa et thoro*;[209] as for adultery, because that **divorce by reason of adultery, cannot dissolve the marriage** *a vinculo matrimonii*, for that the offence is **after** the just and lawfull marriage.[210]

Thomas Comber (1645–1699)

And if we do well consider the words of our Saviour, we shall find this order of our Church[211] to be grounded upon holy Scripture; for though the Jews allowed to Marry again after Divorce for Adultery, yet Jesus correcting this custom, saith, "whosoever shall put away his Wife, saving for the cause of Fornication, causeth her to commit Adultery; and whosoever shall Marry her that is Divorced, committeth Adultery, Matth. v.32. So that he allows Divorce in no cause but that of Fornication, (which is all that Moses also permits under the name of uncleanness, Deut. Xxiv.1.) but **in no case at all doth Christ allow Marriage after Divorce**, calling it plainly Adultery…[212]

Daniel Whitby (1638-1726)

…I incline rather to take the word [*porneia*] in its proper sense for **fornication committed before matrimony**, and found after cohabitation. (1.) Because Christ, speaking of this divorce here and elsewhere, doth never use the world *moicheia*, which signifies adultery, but always *porneia* (Matt. v.32), which word, both among Jews and gentiles, **doth properly**

Miscellaneous Works Of Lancelot Andrewes (Oxford: John Henry Parker, 1854), p.106-108.

[207] I include this because, at the time it was written, it was the law of England and serves as an example of how the English people had rejected the Adultery View.

[208] That is, with the option of remarrying.

[209] That is, *without* the option of remarrying.

[210] Edward Coke (1552-1634), *The Third Part of the Institutes of the Laws of England, Ch. 27* (London: E. & R. Brooke, 1797), p.89.

[211] That is, the Anglican Church.

[212] *The Occasional Offices Of Matrimony, Part 2, Sec. 2* (London: Henry Brome & Robert Clavel, 1679).

<u>import the sin of unmarried persons lying one with another</u>, and so being made one body (1Cor. vi.16): it is not therefore likely that Christ receded from the known and common acceptation of the word.[213]

Hector Davies Morgan (1785–1850)

In the clause of exception it was the undoubted purpose of our Saviour to abridge the facilities of divorce, which the Jews had derived from the word uncleanness in the law of Moses: Deut. xxiv.1. But it is obvious, that if the word *porneia* be of that general sense and signification in which it is interpreted by Grotius and other expositors [to include sexual immorality in general], the explicit purpose of our Lord is defeated by the ambiguity of his language. His clause of exception, thus largely expounded [to be a catch-phrase for all sexual immorality], cannot be supposed to restrict the licence, which was collected from the Mosaic law. This alone is an insuperable objection to the argument of Selden, that *porneia* in the use of the Pharisees is equivalent to any uncleanness.[214]

John Thomas Lord Redesdale (1805-1886)

At length, that which appears to be the true doctrine was generally accepted by the Church, that if a woman is guilty of adultery the husband is justified in putting her away from him, but that **the marriage nevertheless remains indissoluble**.[215]

Johann Joseph Ignaz von Döllinger (1799-1890)

---

[213] *A Critical Commentary And Paraphrase On The Old And New Testament And Apocrypha, Vol. 4, Note On Mt. 19:9* (Philadelphia: Carey & Hart, 1845), p.136.

[214] *The Doctrine and Law of Marriage, Adultery, and Divorce, Vol 2, Appendix 1* (Oxford: J. Parker, 1826), p.400.

[215] *Divorce Commission: Lord Redesdale's Opinion And Statement Of His Reasons For Not Entirely Concurring In The Preceding Report* in *Parliamentary Papers, Vol. 40* (London: Her Majesty's Stationary Office, 1853), p.23. This report is also contained in *First Report Of The Commissioners Appointed By Her Majesty To Enquire Into The Law Of Divorce And More Particularly Into The Mode Of Obtaining Divorces A Vinculo Matimonii* (London: Bradbury And Evans, Whitefriars Printers for Her Majesty's Stationary Office, 1853), p.23 which was part of a compilation in *Reports From Commissioners: 1852-1853, Vol. 1, No. 1604* (no date, no publisher), p.249.

Those who think that, in His two statements about marriage given by Matthew, Christ meant that it was dissolved or made dissoluble by adultery on either side, are compelled (1) to maintain, that the word *porneia* may mean adultery, (2) to find a ground for its being used in a crucial passage instead of the ordinary word *mocheia*, (3) to maintain the principle that one act of adultery on either side *ipso facto* dissolves marriage. These three points require proof. The first assertion must be most emphatically contradicted; ___*porneia* **always means incontinence in the unmarried, never in the N. T. or Septuagint or in profane authors, adultery**___...But, supposing *porneia* could be used for *adulterium*, that does not explain why Christ, or Matthew, should have used the word, where it was essential to define accurately the one ground for dissolution of marriage. Christ more than once uses *moicheia* here; why should He suddenly change the word for "fornication" if He only meant adultery?[216]

Henry Parry Liddon (1829-1890)

Moses had allowed a bill of divorcement; but Christ reaffirms, without exception, the original law, "What God hath joined together let no man put asunder." In other words, He proclaims the indissolubility of the marriage tie. Alluding to the Jewish law, **He rules that if an unacknowledged act of fornication on the part of the woman had preceded the contract, the apparent tie may be dissolved**. I say, the apparent tie; because in reality the contract was vitiated from the first; one of the contracting parties was deceived as to its real terms.[217]

Henry Granville Howard (1815-1860), et al (1857)[218]

---

[216] *The First Age Of Christianity And The Church, Vol. 2, Appendix 3,* Henry Nutcombe Oxenham, Tr. (London: William H. Alen & Co., 1866), p.310-312.

[217] *Sermon XVI: Christ And Human Law, Sec. 2* in *Sermons Preached Before The University Of Oxford, Second Series 1868-1882* (London: Rivingtons, 1883) p.310-312.

[218] 1857 the British Parliament was debating whether to allow people to divorce for the cause of adultery. This attempt to change both the then current law as well as the teachings of Scripture met with resistance from those who took the Bible's teachings on divorce and remarriage seriously. What follows are protest letters written against a change in the law.

[We protest the bill] 1st, Because the Bill contains provisions authorizing in certain cases divorce *a Vinculo Matrimonii* of Christian marriage, and is thus in direct opposition to what our Lord has declared both in His own words and in the unvarying teaching of His Church. –*Signed Henry Granville Howard, William Bernard Petre, Henry Valentine Stafford Jerningham, George Charles Mostyn, Henry Benedict Arundell, & Thomas Alexander Fraser*[219]

Samuel Wilberforce (1805-1873), et al (1857)

[We protest the bill] 1st, Because, in opposition to the word of God, which is embodied in the law of our Church, the Bill sanctions the re-marriage of a divorced husband or wife during the lifetime of the divorced wife or husband. 2ndly, Because in direct contradiction to the plain teaching of our Saviour Christ, the divorced adulteress is permitted to re-marry during the lifetime of her husband…6thly, Because it will lead to the clergy of the Church of England being required to pronounce the blessing of Almighty God on unions condemned by their Church, and repugnant, as many of them believe, to the direct letter of Holy Writ, and to employ at the unions founded on dissolved marriages, from the Marriage Service of the Church of England, language which is in its plain sense inconsistent with the dissolubility of marriage. –*Signed Samuel Wilberforce, Francis Godolphin D'Arcy Osborne, Walter Kerr Hamilton, Horatio Nelson, John Thomas Freeman Mitford, Otway O'Connor Cuffe, & Arthur Hill Trevor*[220]

Isaac Williams (1802–1865)

---

[219] *Protest #883: Against The Marriage Bill* in James E. Thorold Rogers, *A Complete Collection of the Protests of the Lords, Vol. 3: 1826-1874* (Oxford: Clarendon Press, 1875), p.426.

[220] *Protest #884: Against The Marriage Bill* in James E. Thorold Rogers, *A Complete Collection of the Protests of the Lords, Vol. 3: 1826-1874* (Oxford: Clarendon Press, 1875), p.426-427. Sadly, the bill passed and had a markedly negative effect upon the culture of England. John Campbell was one of the politicians most responsible for seeing the bill pass, yet one year after its passage he regretted his decision lamenting that, *"I have been sitting two days in the Divorce Court, and, like Frankenstein, I am afraid of the monster I have called into existence."* (*Life Of John Lord Campbell, Vol. 2*, American Edition [Jersey City, NJ: Frederick D. Linn & Co., 1881], p.432).

'What therefore God hath joined together, let not man put asunder.' Here our Lord sets aside the letter of Holy Scripture, in one case, in the passage in Deuteronomy, (which He speaks of as the command of Moses,) on account of the higher law of Christian holiness and perfection…And therefore this passage in the book of Genesis not only is spoken, as St. Paul says it is, of the Sacramental union betwixt Christ and His Church, but does also signify that marriage is of itself of Divine sanction, and the union formed of God, and necessarily indissoluble as such…for if God hath joined, **man cannot put asunder**.[221]

John Keble (1792-1866)

Therefore **among Christians there can be no such thing as Divorce**. This argument, being purely scriptural, and its conclusion directly in unison with the Law of the Church of England, seems as if it ought to be well considered, by those especially, who think it their duty to be guided in such matters by Scripture alone, and to admit no authoritative interpretation of Scripture but that of the present English Church.[222]

Edward Lowth Badeley (d.1868)

We are consequently driven to the second [method of interpreting the exception clause]; and thus are led to conclude, that the supposed exception of cases of adultery from the prohibition of divorce, which has been inferred from St. Matthew's gospel, **is really no exception at all**; that **the words need not be, and ought not to be, so understood**; and that there is no inconsistency between St. Matthew and the other two Evangelists, in recording our Lord's prohibition.[223]

Civil Code Of Lower Canada (1870)[224]

---

[221] *Thoughts On The Study Of The Holy Gospels* (London: Francis & John Rivington, 1845), p.181-182.

[222] *Sequel Of The Argument Against Immediately Repealing The Laws Which Treat The Nuptial Bond As Indissoluble* (Oxford: J.H. & James Parker, 1857), p.3.

[223] *Considerations On Divorce A Vinculo Matrimonii: In Connexion With Holy Scripture* (London: C.J. Stewart, 1857), p.16. Published pseudonymously as by "A Barrister".

[224] I include this and the other countries below to show that entire nations have based their laws upon a rejection of the adultery view.

Marriage can only be dissolved by the natural death of one of the parties; while both live, it is indissoluble.[225]

William Rollinson Whittingham (1805-1879)

You seem not to have observed, in using Matt, v., 32, that our Lord nowhere at any time recognizes any right of a woman to divorce her husband; nor to have remembered that adultery being punished with death under the Jewish law (so that, as Beza and Wells observe, the case of divorce for actual *adultery* could never legally occur), the word *porneia* should most probably be understood restrictively of **ante-nuptial unchastity discovered after marriage**.[226]

John Henry Blunt (1823-1884)

Thus our Lord confirmed the permission of the Mosaic law in this particular because of the unforgiving character of the Jewish disposition,— *'the hardness of their hearts,'*—but He did not extend the permission to any other case than that of **ante-nuptial unchastity**, or 'fornication.' And thus He swept away at one stroke all those pretences, falsely grounded on the Mosaic law, under which the Jews had so freely used 'bills of divorcement.'[227]

Law Code Of Chile (1893)

Divorce does not dissolve marriage, but merely suspends the joint life of the parties.[228]

Civil Code Of The Argentine Republic (1893)

The divorce sanctioned by this Code consists **only in personal separation** of the married couple without the dissolution of the bonds of

---

[225] Thomas McCord, *The Civil Code of Lower Canada, Second Edition, Book First Of Persons, Title Fifth, Chapter Seventh, No. 185* (Montreal: Dawson, 1870), p.28.

[226] *Letter To The Rev. H.H.H.* in William Francis Brand *Life of William Rollinson Whittingham, Vol. 1* (New York: E. & J. B. Young, 1883), p.488.

[227] *The Sacraments And Sacramental Ordinances Of The Church* (London: Rivingtons, 1867), p.280.

[228] *Civil Marriage Law, Article 19.* Translated and cited in *Reports On The Laws On Marriage And Divorce In Foreign Countries* in *House of Commons Papers, Vol. 70* (London: Her Majesty's Stationary Office, 1894), p.50.

matrimony[229]…A legal marriage **can only be dissolved by the death** of one of the contracting parties.[230]

William Ewart Gladstone (1809-1898)

But we need not shrink from adducing positive ground to show that **no permission of re-marriage is here given**…the supposed exception of St. Matthew is no exception at all so far as concerns the case of re-marriage, but is a simple parenthesis; while the tenor of the passage is restored to perfect harmony and clearness, and St. Matthew stands in entire unison with the other Evangelists.[231]

Petition To The General Convention
Of The Protestant Episcopal Church (1898)

We, the undersigned, bishops and clergy of the Protestant Episcopal Church in the United States—being persuaded that any canon of our church on the question of marriage and divorce ought to be consistent with the words the priest must use when he solemnizes holy matrimony, according to the service contained in the Prayer-Book—do hereby declare it to be our conviction that any legislation on this subject in the way of an amendment to our present canon ought to be based on the following principles:

1. That the marriage law of the church is clearly set forth in the marriage service, namely, that Christian marriage consists in the union of one man with one woman until the union is severed by death.

2. That **this law does not permit the marriage of any person separated by divorce, so long as the former partner is living, whether such person be innocent or guilty**.

(–Signed by 19 bishops and 1,541 priests)[232]

---

[229] *Argentine Marriage Law, Article 64*. Translated and cited in *Reports On The Laws On Marriage And Divorce In Foreign Countries* in *House of Commons Papers, Vol. 70* (London: Her Majesty's Stationary Office, 1894), p.9.

[230] *Article 81.* Ibid, p.10.

[231] *The Bill For Divorce, 1857, Sec. 27 & 40* in *Gleanings of Past Years, 1843-78:Vol. 6: Ecclesiastical* (London: John Murray, 1879), p.63, 72.

[232] The number of signatories is recorded in Henry Yates Satterlee, *The Peace Cross Book: Cathedral of SS. Peter and Paul, Washington* (New York, NY: R.H. Russell, 1899), p.42. The text of the petition is found in G.M.P Bownes, *The Late Convention*

William Crosswell Doane (1832-1913)

...I hold the view that by the teaching of Holy Scripture the marriage bond is indissoluble, that separation is permitted in one case only, but that **no remarriage is possible under any conditions**.[233]

William John Knox Little (c.1839-1918)

If our Lord had said, "Whosoever shall put away his wife, except for the cause of adultery, causeth her to commit adultery," no question could have been raised as to His meaning; in fact, if our Lord meant *moicheia*, why, in a crucial passage, did He go out of His way to say *porneia*? This question has never been answered, and, to my mind, never can be. **Those who try to build teaching upon an apparent exception, to the neglect of the plain assertions of the New Testament, are obliged to use a plain word in a sense which it does not bear, to neglect the whole bearing of the passage, and to treat our Lord's utterances, and those of His great Apostle, as being quite inconsistent with one another**. I maintain, therefore, that the teaching of the English Church—following the tradition of the Western Church, and the best traditions of the early Eastern Church—as to *the absolute indissolubility of the marriage bond except by death,* is entirely consonant with the plain meaning of the words of our Lord.[234]

Azusa Street Meetings (1906-1936)[235]

Of The Protestant Episcopal Church in *The Catholic World, Vol. 68: October, 1898 to March, 1899* (New York, NY: The Office Of The Catholic World, 1899), p.259.

[233] *Divorce And Remarriage* in John Vyrnwy Morgan, ed. *Theology At The Dawn Of The Twentieth Century: Essays On The Present Status of Christianity And Its Doctrines* (Boston, Small, Maynard & Co., 1901), p.348.

[234] *Marriage And Divorce: The Doctrine Of The Church Of England* in *Contemporary Review, Vol. 68: July to December 1895* (London: Isbister & Co., 1895), p.264.

[235] The Azusa Street meetings (often referred to as the Azusa Street Revival) are considered by Pentecostals to be the birth of the modern Pentecostal movement. Denominations such as the Assemblies of God trace their roots back to the services which took place on Azusa Street in Los Angeles, California. Pentecostal Christians refer back to the Azusa meetings as an example of what all Pentecostalism should be today. Interestingly, they will often refer to it as "the greatest move of the Holy Spirit since Pentecost". With such a high regard for the

I. To marry a second companion while a former lives is adultery--sin--and is forbidden (Mark 7:2,3; 10:11,12). II. To marry a person who has a living companion is adultery--sin--and is forbidden (Matt. 5:23; Luke 16:18; 1 John 3:4). 1. The above is the law of Christ, and sin is the transgression of the law (1 John 3:4)...III. Men who have a knowledge of the teachings of Christ's law regarding marriage, and then with that knowledge marry a second living companion, or a divorced wife or husband while their former companion lives, wilfully transgress the law and are guilty before God of sin--adultery--and must forsake their sin (1 John 1:9; 3:4). If we confess our sins He will pardon us. All such unscriptural marriages must be dissolved to get clear from the sinful state of adultery (Prov. 28:13; Isa. 1:16, 17; Gal. 5:19-21; 1 Cor. 6:9, 10.) IV. If men entered the unscriptural marriages, even though ignorant of the written law, yet condemned by the law of their conscience, such are not clear before God (Rom. 2:12, 14-16)...Under the New Testament, no court on earth should dissolve the marriage relation (Mark 10:2-9; Matt. 19:5-6). 6. Under the New Testament, husband and wife are bound together for life. **Death alone severs the marriage tie**. 7. Under the New Testament, there is but one cause for which a man can put away his wife. 8. After a man has lawfully put away his wife, or a wife has lawfully put away her husband, **they are positively forbidden to marry again until the former companion is dead** (Mark 10:11, 12; Luke 16:18; Rom. 7:2, 3)[236]

Lambeth Conference Of 1908

When an innocent person has, by means of a court of law, divorced a spouse for adultery, and desires to enter into another contract of marriage, **it is undesirable that such a contract should receive the blessing of the Church**.[237]

Azusa services it is unclear as to why much of modern day Pentecostalism would reject what the Azusa Meetings said the Holy Spirit had told them to teach concerning divorce and remarriage.

[236] William J. Seymour *The Doctrines And Discipline Of The Azusa Street Apostolic Faith Mission Of Los Angeles (The Complete Azusa Street Library), Marriage And Family: Unscriptural Marriage, Separation* Larry Edward Martin, ed. (Joplin, MO: Christian Life Books, 2000), p.119-122.

[237] *Resolution 40, "The Lambeth Conference Official Website"* at http://www.lambethconference.org/resolutions/1908/1908-40.cfm

Morgan Dix (1827-1908)

In the Church there have been, from of old, a stringent and a less stringent view. The stringent rule is this: that, though the married may be separated so as to live apart when they can not live together in peace, yet are they still man and wife; and no new matrimonial relation can be formed. They may come back to each other; to strange flesh they can not go. And I think that must have been what the Lord meant, and that it ought to be the rule of the Church.[238]

William Lefroy (1836-1909)

And accordingly the Christian Church has ever held that the mind of Christ is that marriage is indissoluble. Life-long monogamy is the condition supposed and enjoined by Holy Scripture...So far, then, we claim that the teaching of Holy Scripture is the indissolubility of the marriage bond: the union is essential, its duration is permanent.[239]

Herbert Mortimer Luckock (1833–1909)

Such, then, are the circumstances under which Christ spoke on the subject of divorce, and we submit that, when carefully considered, His words leave little doubt that in what He intended to apply to the Christian Church, **He gave no sanction to any divorce which was supposed to carry with it a right to marry again**, before at least death had severed the bond; but maintained for all its members the absolute indissolubility of the marriage tie.[240]

General Council Of The Assemblies Of God (1921)[241]

---

[238] *Lectures On The Calling Of A Christian Woman And Her Training To Fulfil It, Delivered During The Season Of Lent, AD 1883, Lecture 5: Divorce* (New York, NY: D. Appleton & Co., 1883), p.140.

[239] *Divorce* in *The Church And Life Of To-day*, p.42-43. Cited in Henry John Wilkins *The History Of Divorce And Re-marriage For English Churchmen* (London: Longmans, Green & Co., 1910), p.45.

[240] *The History Of Marriage: Jewish And Christian, In Relation To Divorce And Certain Forbidden Degrees* (London: Longmans, Green & Co., 1894), p.71.

[241] This, in effect, was a rejection of the Adultery View by the early Assemblies of God denomination. Christians who did divorce over adultery were counseled to remain single and Assembly of God ministers were forbidden from performing a marriage ceremony for a person who had divorced because of adultery.

Whereas, low standards on marriage and divorce are very hurtful to individuals, to the family, and to the cause of Christ, therefore be it recommended that in the future we discourage divorce by all lawful means and teaching, and that we shall positively disapprove in the future of Christians getting divorce for any cause except for fornication or adultery (Matt. 19: 9); and that **we recommend the remaining single of all divorced Christians**, and that they pray God so to keep them in purity and peace…And as a means of making the above more effective, **we further advise our Pentecostal ministry not to perform a marriage ceremony between any believer and a divorced person whose former companion is still living**.[242]

Oscar Daniel Watkins (1848-1926)

The results of the investigations contained in those chapters may be here anticipated in the brief statement that the Divine institution of marriage, as restored in the Christian Church, admits neither Polygamy **nor such Divorce as concedes re-marriage**…From what has already been said in previous chapters it will have appeared that the answer which as a result of this investigation we shall feel justified in giving is the answer that **marriage is indissoluble in its own essential character, and that divorce from the bond of marriage is always and in every case inadmissible**.[243]

Duncan Convers (1851-1929)

Notice the word used by Christ in the passages given by St. Matthew. It is *porneia*, **a word certainly used of incontinence in the unmarried**; but where is it ever used of incontinence with a single paramour freely consented to by the married woman?…In taking *porneia*, in the passages in St. Matthew, to exclude "adultery," we are reading it so as to make Christ's use of language consistent with itself, agreeing with the use of St. Matthew xv. 19 and St. Mark vii. 21. Here we have the two words contrasted; and the same contrast between "fornicators" and "adulterers" is found in Hebrews xiii. 5. Whenever Christ meant more than mere "fornication," either *moicheia* or *achatharsia* is joined to it. And the same is

---

[242] *Combined Minutes Of The General Council Of The Assemblies Of God, Minutes 1921*, under the section entitled *Marriage And Divorce*, (no publication information in printed booklet), p.22.

[243] *Holy Matrimony* (London: Rivington, Percival & Co., 1895), p.110, 152.

true of all New Testament writers…If Christ meant by *porneia* to include adultery as well as fornication discovered after marriage, why did He not use both words conjointly as He usually did? Besides, no Greek scholar has ever yet suggested that *porneia* was the exact synonyme of *moicheia*; **even our opponents hold that it includes ante-nuptial unchastity**.[244]

Walker Gwynne (1845-1931)

But putting these arguments aside as non-essential or inconclusive, the one supreme fact that stands out as strongly and clearly in S. Matthew as in S. Mark and S. Luke is that "whosoever shall marry *any woman* that is divorced" (a single word in the Greek, *apolelumenen*), whether for fornication or any other cause, "committeth adultery." But if the bond is *really* broken by adultery, fornication, or any other cause, it follows logically that *both* parties are free. In that case however a difficulty arises as to why our Lord should forbid remarriage to the guilty party, as He does, while He allows it by His silence, as some would contend, to the innocent. The only possible explanation of this apparent inconsistency is that **the inference from His silence is wrong. The bond is *not* broken, but only profaned; neither party is free, and the prohibition applies equally to both innocent and guilty.**[245]

Henry Edwin Savage (1855-1939)

In dealing with it however our Lord did not range Himself with any of the disputants…He taught that divorce in itself is a breach of the marriage bond, and therefore on no account allowable, except only for the one cause specified in the Law. **That cause was prenuptial unchastity**.[246]

Jerry Miles Humphrey (b. 1872-d.unk.)

Every honest and level-headed Bible reader will agree that Matt. 19:9 is the only passage in the whole Bible that seems to give grounds for divorce parties to remarry. Of course Matt. 5:32 gives grounds to put away the unclean party, but does not say either party can marry again.

---

[244] *Marriage And Divorce In The United States: As They Are And As They Ought To Be* (J. B. Lippincott Co., 1889), p.208-210.

[245] *Primitive Worship And The Prayer Book* (New York, NY: Longmans, Green & Co., 1917), p.320.

[246] *The Gospel Of The Kingdom* (London: Longmans, Green & Co., 1910), p.112.

We also agree that it does not say they cannot. But the Bible says so in four or five other places which we will mention later. We often meet people who say that Mark, Luke, Romans and I Corinthians are to be read in connection with Matt. 19:9; i. e., the exception is to be recognized in reading those passages. But the safer way, to my mind, would be to accept the testimony of the three writers in preference to accepting the testimony of one against the three. Jesus says, "In the mouth of two or three witnesses every word is established."[247]

Constitution of South Carolina (1895-1949)

Divorces from the bonds of matrimony shall not be allowed in this state.[248]

Frederic H. Chase (1853-1925)

Now I venture to say that, when a Jew read the exceptive clause in St. Matthew, a passage in Deuteronomy would at once have come into his mind. It is there (Deut. xxii. 13-21) provided that, if a man marries and after marriage discovers that the woman is not a virgin, he may make his accusation against her known. If (according to the evidence prescribed) "this thing be true," then the woman shall be stoned…Christ, then, if this interpretation be true, substituting nullification of the marriage for stoning, allowed that, if a woman had committed fornication before marriage, her husband might put her away. In my judgment, this is the natural and most probable interpretation.[249]

Jane Walker (1859-1938)

Divorce and subsequent re-marriage in pre-Reformation days were only allowed on grounds existing before the contract was entered into. (There seems good reason for the belief that **our Lord's words as recorded by St. Matthew refer to prenuptial unchastity**.)[250]

---

[247] *A Word Of Warning On Divorce-Marriage* (Philadelphia, PA: Gospel Words & Music, no date).

[248] *Article 17, Sec. 3*. Cited in *The Pacific Reporter, Vol. 142: August 31-October 12, 1914* (St. Paul: West Publishing Co., 1914), p.236.

[249] *What Did Christ Teach About Divorce?* (London: Society For Promoting Christian Knowledge, 1921), p.27-28.

[250] *A Memorandum On Divorce* in *The Challenger, July 5, 1918*. Cited in A. Maude Royden *Sex and Common Sense* (New York, NY: G. P. Putnam's Sons, 1922), p.210.

Paul Bull (1864-1942)

The exceptive clauses in S. Matthew undoubtedly refer to the discovery at marriage that the betrothed has not been faithful, and in no way refer to adultery after marriage, nor permit divorce with remarriage...(1) The word used in both these passages is "fornication" and not "adultery." (2) Those who first heard or read the Gospel would know quite well that the clause referred to **prenuptial sin** in one who was espoused.[251]

Frederick C. Grant (1891-1974)

Porneia is simply not adultery but fornication, i.e. either "harlotry" or **pre-marital sexual indulgence**...it is still clearly affirmed that to put away one's wife and marry another it to commit adultery; the only apparent exception is when the charge of harlotry or fornication — i.e. **"pre-martial sex experience,"** as we call it — has been proved.[252]

Glenn Griffith (1894–1976)

Some say that if husband or wife commits adultery, he or she is dead to the innocent party, who then is free to marry again. NO, friend, the death that releases those bound by the marriage relation is not a theoretical, typical, or symbolic death; but it is a genuine physical death. And just as we are freed from the law of sin only by the death of Christ (Rom. 7:4), so we are freed from the law of marriage only by the death of our companion.[253]

William Fisher-Hunter (b.1899-d.unk.)

Believing the crux in the whole case of a Christian getting a divorce on the ground of adultery is wrapped up in the misuse of one word "fornication" I have gone to great lengths to show that when the term is interpreted in the light of the statute of divorce as given by Moses and by

---

[251] *Marriage And Divorce* (London: Society For Promoting Christian Knowledge, 1924), p.8, 10.

[252] *The Mind Of Christ On Marriage* in *Five Essays On Marriage* (no city of pub.: Cloister Press, no date of pub.), p.36-37.

[253] *Until Death Do Us Part* (Dundee, Il: Metropolitan Press, 1958), p.23.

the rule of accumulative evidence, __it cannot honestly be made to mean adultery__.[254]

Code Of Canon Law Of The Roman Catholic Church (1983)[255]

A marriage that is ratified and consummated can be dissolved by no human power and by no cause, except death.[256]

Southeastern Mennonite Conference (1983)

Scripturally, there is nothing which breaks the marriage bond except death. __The act of adultery does not dissolve the marriage bond,__ although it decidedly affects the quality of a marriage relationship and leaves a permanent scar on the persons involved. A legal document called divorce, from God's point of view, does not break the marriage bond, else remarriage would not be adultery. Even the conversion of one of two unbelieving married partners does not dissolve the marriage bond. __If the unbelieving partner should leave, the marriage bond continues__.[257]

And it is not just writers from the past. There are contemporary writers who have rejected the Adultery View although their books do not

---

[254] *The Divorce Problem Fully Discussed And A Scriptural Solution, First Edition* (Waynesboro, PA: MacNeish Publishers, 1952), p.74.

[255] To my knowledge, only two of the writers quoted after the Reformation in this section were Roman Catholic. This book is geared towards Evangelicals but I include the Roman Catholic Church's official rejection of the Adultery View here to show that if all of Christendom is taken into consideration then the majority have rejected the idea that adultery justifies divorce and remarriage. Experiencing an 11.54% increase in membership between 2000 and 2008, with 1.16 billion members as of 2008 and existing as the largest denomination in the United States they serve as proof that a church or denomination can grow even if it will not allow its members to remarry in the case of adultery.

[256] Canon 1141. Canons 1097-1098 indicate that a marriage based upon a fraud that could affect the sexual life of the two partners (which would include the idea of concealing prenuptial sin) can be annulled: "A person contracts [marriage] invalidly who enters marriage __inveigled by deceit, perpetrated in order to secure consent, concerning some quality of the other party__, which of its very nature can seriously disrupt the partnership of __conjugal life__."

[257] *Statement of Position on Divorce and Remarriage.* Officially adopted as a statement of position and policy on June 24, 1983, by the Southeastern Mennonite Conference.

seem to have been as popular as those advocating the Adultery View. These include John Coblentz,[258] Joseph Webb,[259] Casey Whitaker,[260] Robert Ephrata,[261] S. Flinchum,[262] David Engelsma,[263] Omar E. Lee,[264] Arne Rudvin,[265] Barry Gritters,[266] Dirk E. T. Evenhuis,[267] Stephen Wilcox,[268] Cheryl Chrisman[269], Michael Whennen,[270] Tim Corban,[271] Bob Mutch,[272] Joe Fogle,[273] Leslie McFall,[274] Josiahs Scott,[275] Sean Bonitto,[276] and Rick Friedrich[277].

I realize that the above list of quotations was rather lengthy, yet I felt it necessary to include all of it to reassure those who are having doubts about the Adultery View that there have always been people who

---

[258] *Marriage, Divorce And Remarriage* (Harrisonburg, VA: Christian Light Publications, 1992).

[259] *Divorce and Remarriage: The Trojan Horse Within the Church* (Longwood, FL: Xulon Press, 2008). *Till Death Do Us Part* (Webb Ministries, Inc., 2003).

[260] *Have You Not Read?* (Fredericksburg OH: Faith View Books, 2009).

[261] *Christian Care & Concern For Marriage, Divorce, And Remarriage* (FBF Missions, 2008).

[262] *Adultery In The Church* (Landmark Archiving and Multimedia Publishing Co, 2004).

[263] *Until Death Do Us Part* (South Holland, IL: South Holland Protestant Reformed Evangelism Committee, 2005). *Marriage And Divorce* (South Holland, IL: South Holland Protestant Reformed Church, no pub. date).

[264] *Is Divorce And Remarriage Biblical?* in *Holiness Data Ministries CD-ROM*, file # HDM0809, digital edition 11/02/98, (no original pub. info., no original pub.date).

[265] *"What Jesus Said About Divorce And Remarriage"* in *Dagen, 1994*.

[266] *The Family: Foundations Are Shaking* (Hudsonville, MI: Hudsonville Protestant Reformed Church, no pub. date).

[267] www.holymatrimony.org

[268] www.marriagedivorce.com

[269] www.cadz.net

[270] www.wisereaction.org

[271] www.amatterofsalvation.com

[272] www.morechristlike.com

[273] www.theoslog.com

[274] Former Research Fellow at Tyndale House Library, Cambridge, England. His personal website is at http://www.btinternet.com/~lmf12/ .

[275] www.trueconnection.org

[276] www.internationaldeliveranceministries.org

[277] www.truthinheart.com

rejected that interpretation from the time of Jesus until the present. We just do not hear much about an alternative view today because the Adultery View, promoted by many of our modern Bible translations, has become so enormously popular. But keep in mind, however, that just because something is popular, that does not make it correct. Indeed, the truth is rarely popular (Lk 6:26).

What the Bible Clearly Teaches About Divorce And Remarriage

As one studies the issue of divorce and remarriage it becomes clear that the related Bible passages fall into either one of two categories—*Clear-cut, straight to the point passages* and *unclear, ambiguous passages*. Strangely, when individuals are seeking to discover what the Bible teaches about remarriage after a divorce, the *clear passages* are usually ignored in favor of discussions upon the *unclear passages* in an attempt to see if they allow remarriage after divorce or not and, if so, under what conditions. This heavy emphasis upon the *unclear passages* as opposed to the *clear teachings* of the New Testament should lead us to ask two fundamental questions—*1.) What is the purpose of the clear passages?* and *2.) Is it safe to base a moral decision upon an unclear passage when you have a clear passage which tells you the heart of God on a particular issue?*

Our inquiry into the real meaning of Matthew's exception clause would not be complete without looking at the *clear* New Testament passages on divorce and remarriage, for surely, they must have some bearing upon its meaning.

The Clear Teachings Of The New
Testament Upon Divorce And Remarriage

And he said unto them, 'Whoever shall put away his wife, and marry another, commits adultery against her.' Mk 10:11	According to Jesus' teaching in Mark, if a man divorces his wife and enters into a marriage with another woman he commits the sin of adultery against his first wife.
And if a woman shall put away her husband, and be married to another, she commits adultery. Mk	He continues by indicating that if a woman divorces her husband and enters into a marriage with another

10:12	man she also commits the sin of adultery against her first husband.
Whoever puts away his wife, and marries another, commits adultery... Lk 16:18a	According to Jesus' teaching in Luke, if a man divorces his wife and marries another he commits the sin of adultery against his first wife.
...and whoever marries her that is put away from her husband commits adultery. Lk 16:18b	Jesus continues his teaching upon divorce and remarriage by reminding his listeners that if a man decides to marry a woman who has been divorced by her husband then he commits the sin of adultery by doing so.
And unto the married I command, yet not I, but the Lord, 'Let not the wife depart from her husband (but if she does depart, let her remain unmarried, or be reconciled to her husband)...' 1Co 7:10-11a	Paul here instructs the Corinthian Christians that a wife is not to leave or divorce her husband but if this does happen then she is to either *remain single* for the rest of her life or *be reconciled* back to her husband.
...and let not the husband put away his wife. 1Co 7:11b	Paul continues by instructing his male readers that they have been commanded by Jesus to *not* divorce their wives.
The wife is bound by the law as long as her husband lives; but if her husband is dead, she is at liberty to be married to whom she will; only in the Lord. 1Co 7:39	Paul concludes his instructions to the Corinthian Christians by telling them that a wife is "bound" to her first husband until he dies and that it is only *after* his death that a woman is free to get married for a second time.

These are the *clear teachings* of the New Testament upon the issue of divorce and remarriage. They are very plain and extremely direct. Anyone who reads the *clear passages* will come to the conclusion that God does not allow divorce and remarriage from a validly entered into marriage. It is surprising that for an issue which has the potential to determine whether one spends an eternity burning in hell that the *unclear passages* on this issue would receive the most attention and be oftentimes given the most priority by persons who are making a decision as to whether to remarry after experiencing a divorce. This should lead all thinking Christians to ask two fundamental questions:

1.) What is the purpose of the clear passages? In other words, were they put there for a reason? Does God expect us to ignore His *clear* teachings to us regarding divorce and remarriage in favor of *unclear* passages? Why did God put these passages here in such a clear-cut and direct way if He intended to reverse them in other passages?

2.) Is it safe to base a moral decision upon an *unclear* passage when you have a *clear* passage which tells you the heart of God on a particular issue? In other words, is it wise to make a decision that could determine where one will spend all of eternity based upon an unclear verse when one has a clear verse telling us how God wants us to behave in a particular situation?

Let's Dig Deeper

Let's take our inquiry into the *clear passages* a little further. Jesus says that in each of the above instances if a person enters into a remarriage state then he or she "commits adultery". The question is how do they "commit" adultery. Is it once (at the time when they first enter into the new marriage) or do they "commit" adultery *continuously* so long as they are in the new marriage? Looking at the Greek in these passages gives us the answer to this question. In each of these passages the Greek verb for "commits adultery" is in the *present tense*. The present tense in Greek generally indicates that something happens continuously in an on-going manner. When a Greek verb is written in the present tense it implies that it has continued from the moment that it began up until the

113

present and is still continuing. This understanding of how the Greek present tense normally operates is well attested to by Greek scholars:

"The present tense refers to what is usually described as *continuous action*, sometimes called linear or *ongoing action*. It is action that began at some point in the undefined past and has not ended. It is "present" in the sense that it *continues into the present*. The picture that the present tense provides is of *something occurring now*. It designates action that is right now *continuing* as it began." (Joseph Webb, Robert Kysar, *Greek For Preachers*, Chalice Press: 2002, p.46)

"The present tense is basically linear or durative, *ongoing* in its kind of action. The durative notion may be expressed graphically by an unbroken line (--), since the action is simply *continuous*." (James Hewitt, *New Testament Greek*, Hendrickson Publishers: 1986, p.13)

"The Greek Present corresponds more closely in meaning to the English Present *Continuous* than to the Present Simple." (John William Wenham, Henry Preston Vaughan Nunn, *The Elements of New Testament Greek*, Cambridge Univ. Press: 1991, p.27)

"The Present Tense Stem expresses *continuous* (or *durative*) action..." (John Thompson, *A Greek Grammar: Accidence and Syntax For Schools and Colleges*, John Murray: 1902, p.314)

"The present tense is used of present time and has a *continuous* type of action in view." (J. Lyle Story, Cullen I. K. Story, Peter Allen Miller, *Greek To Me*, Xulon Press: 2002, p.14)

"The present expresses *repetition, habit, continuance*; the aorist, a single irrevocable act of surrender." (William Webster, *The Syntax And Synonyms Of The Greek Testament*, Gilbert and Rivington: 1864, p.89)

"The Present marks *continuity*; the Aorist, *a single act*; the Future (very rare in the New Testament), *intention or futurity*; and the Perfect, *a completed act*." (Samuel Gosnell Green, *Handbook To The Grammar Of The Greek Testament: Together With A Complete Vocabulary*, Fleming H. Revell: 1886, p.324)

"The present tense usually denotes **_continuous_** kind of action. It shows 'action **_in progress_**' or '**_a state of persistence_**.' When used in the indicative mood, the present tense denotes action taking place or going on in the present time. (*Greek Verbs (Shorter Definitions)*, www.ntgreek.org[278])

The implication of Jesus' words, as attested to by the above Greek scholars, is that if two individuals enter into a marriage that Jesus describes as being adulterous they _continuously_ commit adultery _every time_ that they have intercourse.

Imaginary Aoristic Presents

Such an understanding of Jesus' teachings on divorce and remarriage, undoubtedly, makes a lot of people feel uncomfortable. So, in an attempt to smooth over what Jesus *actually said* some interpreters have tried to maintain that the present tenses in these passages are what are referred to as "aoristic presents". No study of this issue would be complete without examining the aoristic present as anyone who studies the topic of divorce and remarriage is going to run into this term. In Greek, the "aorist tense" is a way of writing a verb so that it will be understood to describe an act whose duration is *indefinite* in nature:

> "The constant characteristic of the Aorist tense in all of its moods, including the participle, is that it represents the action denoted by it indefinitely; *i.e.* simply as an event, neither on the one hand picturing it in progress, nor on the other affirming the existence of its result. The name *indefinite* as thus understood is therefore applicable to the tense in all of its uses."[279]

The "aorist tense" can be used to describe an event that happens, but for which it cannot be said exactly how long it did or will happen. It is *indefinite.* As noted above, the "present tense" is normally used to refer

---

[278] http://www.ntgreek.org/learn_nt_greek/verbs1.htm#INDICATIVE, accessed September 23, 2011.

[279] Ernest De Witt Burton, *Syntax Of The Moods And Tenses In New Testament Greek* (Chicago, IL: University Press Of Chicago, 1896), p.16.

to an act whose duration is *definite* in the sense that it is *continuous* in nature.

Sometimes, when a Greek verb is written in the "present tense" it is clear that the action being described is going to continue but that it is not going to continue forever. When this happens the term "aoristic present" is used to describe that verb. An example of this is found in Agrippa's giving of permission for Paul to speak in Acts 26:1.

Then Agrippa said unto Paul, You *are being permitted* (aoristic present) to speak for yourself.[280]

When Agrippa spoke to Paul he told him in the *present tense* that he was "being permitted" to speak, yet it is clear that Paul's permission will not continue forever. Agrippa will eventually get tired and go to bed and Paul will no longer have permission to speak to him. The action of the verb was *continuous* in the sense that Paul was able to continue exercising Agrippa's permission but that permission to speak would eventually come to an end, although we have no way of *defining* when that permission will cease to continue. This is why A. T. Robertson points out in his *A Grammar Of The Greek New Testament, Vol. 1* that:

The aoristic present = <u>undefined action in the present</u>, as aoristic past (ind.) = undefined action in the past.[281]

An "aoristic present" is action occurring in the present but without being defined as to how long it will occur. Its duration is "undefined".

Having given a basic understanding of the "aoristic present" let us now examine how it is sometimes applied to Jesus' teachings regarding the adultery of remarriages and why it is *incorrect* to apply it to these passages.

When people advocate that Jesus' adultery clauses are "aoristic presents" they always maintain that the action of "committing adultery" occurs at the either the time of the second marriage ceremony (i.e. the

---

[280] Author's own translation.

[281] *A Grammar Of The Greek New Testament In The Light Of Historical Research, Vol. 1* (New York, NY: Hodder & Stoughton, George H. Doran Co., 1914), p.865.

remarriage event) or at the consummation (first sexual act) of the remarriage. In their way of thinking the "adultery" only occurs at either the time and place of the second nuptials or at the time and place of the second consummation and afterwards *ceases to continue*. This is how all articles and books that I have read use the "aoristic present" in their interpretations of Jesus' divorce teachings. The following steps will explain how those who feel that the divorce passages are "aoristic presents" should be interpreted.

1. Man is married
2. Man divorces wife and remarries
3. Man commits adultery in partaking in another marriage ceremony/consummating the second marriage
4. Man ceases committing adultery after marriage ceremony/first consummation is over

The problem with this way of using the "aoristic present" is that it violates the basic reason for which an "aoristic present" is used. An "aoristic present" is used to describe an event which is *undefined* in nature. By *defining* the adultery to be taking place only at the second marriage ceremony or the first consummation the proponents of this view are contradicting themselves. If they can *define* when the adultery begins and ends, then this could not be a usage of the "aoristic present". Remember, according to A. T. Robertson's Greek grammar, "The aoristic present = *undefined* action in the present". This is why I entitled this section as "Imaginary Aoristic Presents". If one can define when the event occurred (which proponents of this interpretation claim to be able to do) then it cannot be an example of the "aoristic present".

When one wants to truly understand what words in a sentence mean they must take into consideration the context of where those words appear. Examining the entire context of one of Jesus' divorce and remarriage passages will give us a clearer understanding of how long the adultery lasts. In Luke 16:18 Jesus declares:

Whoever <u>**puts away**</u> **(*present continuous tense*) his wife, and** <u>**marries**</u> **(*present continuous tense*) another,** <u>**commits adultery**</u> **(*present continuous tense*) and whoever** <u>**marries**</u> **(*present**

117

continuous tense) her that is put away from her husband <u>commits adultery</u> *(present continuous tense)*.

When one looks at Jesus' teachings on divorce and remarriage in Luke 16:18 it becomes clear that the action of committing adultery is actually connected to the two other actions of "putting away one's wife" and "entering into another state of marriage" all of which are in the Greek *present continuous tense*. When one looks at the Greek of this passage it will be seen that, because of the use of the present tense, this passage is really saying:

> **"Whoever** <u>*continues to put away his wife*</u>**, and** <u>*enters into a continuous and ongoing state of marriage*</u> **with another,** <u>*commits adultery continuously*</u>**: and whoever** <u>*enters into a continuous and ongoing state of marriage*</u> **with her that is put away from her husband** <u>*commits adultery continuously*</u>**."**

The act of committing adultery is dependent upon the two acts of putting away one's wife and entering into another marriage relationship. In other words, *so long as* one "puts away his wife" and stays in a relationship where he "is married to someone else" he commits adultery. We fail to see this understanding of the passage because we think of divorce and remarriage as one time events. We can name the dates on which our divorce was decreed by a judge and upon which our new marriage took place. This is because we think of "divorce" and "marriage" as nouns (things), not verbs (actions). People really miss what Jesus was saying in this passage because they are thinking of the first two actions as nouns, when in reality they are present continuous verbs. When a person "puts away his wife" he does not do it just on the day that he divorces her. He *continues* to put her away for however long he refuses to be reconciled with her. And when a man "marries another" he does not do it just on the day that he has the ceremony. He *continues* to be in a state of marriage with her for however long they live as a married couple. This is the key to determining how long the adultery lasts.

<u>Continuing</u> To Put Away One's Wife + <u>Continuing</u> To Live In A Marital State With A New Woman = <u>Continuing</u> To Commit Adultery

This is the most consistent and common sense understanding of how adultery works yet we fail to realize it because we do not take into consideration that each of these three verbs are interconnected. If one part of the equation is taken away, the whole answer changes. If the man's first wife dies and he is, therefore, no longer able to put her away he ceases to commit adultery. Likewise, if he ceases to live in a marital state with the new woman, he also ceases to commit adultery. The three parts of the equation all go together.

I fear that the "aoristic present" method of interpreting Jesus' teachings on divorce and remarriage was born out of convenience rather than conviction. It provides a convenient way of getting around the very inconvenient teachings of Jesus regarding the continual nature of a remarriage's adultery but it is not founded upon solid Greek grammar.

The idea that one could enter into an unscriptural divorce and remarriage without being in a continual state of adultery became popular in the 20th century as a response to the large number of divorces and remarriages that were occurring. In all of my studies upon this subject all major theologians that I have found before the 20th century maintained that those who entered into unscriptural remarriages (however they defined them) were in a state of *continuous* and *perpetual* adultery. To say that individuals who have divorced and remarried without the approval of Scripture are not committing adultery is to reject 1900 years of Christian interpretation of how unscriptural remarriages are viewed by God.

Thoughts On The Pauline Privilege

No discussion of divorce and remarriage would be complete without examining what is often referred to as the "Pauline Privilege". Together with the Adultery View it has become part of the official position of the mainline Evangelical church. It is based upon Paul's statement in 1Corinthians 7:13-15 which reads:

And to the woman who has a husband that does not believe: if he is pleased to dwell with her, let her stay with him. For the unbelieving husband is sanctified by the wife, and the unbelieving wife is sanctified by the husband: otherwise your children would be unclean; but now they are holy. But if the unbelieving departs, let him depart. A brother or a sister is not under bondage in such cases: but God has called us to peace.

Those who hold to the Pauline Privilege believe that in a marriage between a Christian and a non-Christian (unbeliever) that this passage is teaching that if the unbelieving spouse departs, then the believing spouse is no longer under bondage to the marriage covenant and is, therefore, free to remarry. Because most marriages in the United States are between professing Christians (as evidenced by the high number of marriages that take place in Christian churches before Christian ministers) those who hold to the Pauline Privilege have interpreted it to mean that in any case where a spouse is abandoned the innocent spouse is free to remarry. They reason that no true believer would abandon their spouse and, therefore, if one spouse abandons the other it is evidence that they were not a true believer and the Pauline Privilege would go into effect.

Interestingly, though this interpretation has been around for centuries, it was not really popular among most Protestant denominations before the American divorce surge. Before the 1970's there were a few denominations who embraced it, but most who allowed remarriage only did so when adultery had taken place. All that changed when the states began changing their divorce laws to allow for no-fault divorce. After the introduction of no-fault divorce a husband or wife could abandon their spouse for no reason at all and churches now found themselves in the predicament of how to handle the high number of abandoned spouses who either had remarried or wanted to remarry and at the same time enjoy the privileges of church membership. The "Pauline Privilege" seemed to provide an easy way out of a very inconvenient situation. The problem, however, is that this way of defining what Paul meant directly contradicts what Jesus taught regarding the ability of an innocent, abandoned spouse to remarry. In two places Jesus specifically said that the abandoned spouse *did not* have the privilege of remarrying.

And I say unto you, whoever shall put away his wife, except it be for fornication, and shall marry another, commits adultery: and **whoever marries her which is put away** does commit adultery. Mt 19:9

120

Whoever puts away his wife, and marries another, commits adultery and **whoever marries her that is put away** from her husband commits adultery. Lk 16:18

In both of these passages Jesus is describing situations for which the modern interpretation of the Pauline Privilege would say that they could remarry, yet Jesus says that they *cannot*. In both of these passages Jesus is describing a wife who has been abandoned by her husband (put away) because he no longer wants to be with her. Surely, no true believer would do that. Yet, despite being abandoned by a husband whose behavior shows him to be an unbeliever, Jesus declares that if the wife remarries then she is sinning (committing adultery). This is why the modern interpretation of the Pauline Privilege is *flawed*. It completely contradicts what Jesus taught regarding divorce and remarriage in the case of abandonment. Those who try to justify remarriage based upon 1Corinthians 7:13-15 must do so (and can only do so) by ignoring what Jesus taught about this *very type* of circumstance. If Paul said something *unclearly* that seemed to contradict what Jesus had taught, common sense tells us to interpret it in the light of what Jesus said *clearly*.

So, what then is 1Corinthians 7:13-15 talking about? Well, we can be pretty certain that it is not talking about the freedom to remarry because in the very same chapter Paul lays down the principle that, no matter what kind of "bondage" he was referring to here, a woman was "bound" to her husband for his entire life (even if they separated).

The wife is bound by the law as long as her husband lives; but if her husband is dead, she is at liberty to be married to whom she will; only in the Lord. 1Co 7:39

So, whatever the "bondage" here was that Paul had in mind, it didn't have anything to do with a wife being able to remarry if her unbelieving husband departed. Such an interpretation requires one to cause Paul to contradict himself here within just a few verses space. More than likely, Paul uses the term "bondage" to refer to the stress of the mixed marriage situation between the believer and the unbeliever. In a pagan setting a spouse who was not a believer may put pressure upon their believing spouse to worship the old gods or to renounce Christ. The believer, knowing that God wants them to do everything within their power to save the marriage may feel pressured to give into this temptation in order to preserve the family. Surely some early mixed marriages resulted in the unbeliever departing and telling the believer that they would not return unless they gave up their new religion. What Paul appears to be saying in 1Corinthians 7:13-15 is that one does not need to feel "under bondage" to renounce Christ in order to please their mate. If their mate wants to leave, let them leave if it is going to come down to them compromising their obedience to Christ. But just a few verses later Paul also reminds them to remember that if they do leave "the wife is bound by the law *as long as her husband lives*" (1Co 7:39).

Going With The Evidence

As I spent the past several years thinking over this issue I was faced with the fact that I was going to have to make a decision. I had preached the Adultery View for years. It was very popular in churches and many Christians just seemed to take it for granted that this was the message that Jesus wanted the world to know. However, the more I looked at the evidence the less likely the Adultery View seemed to me. Greek literature before, at the time of and after the New Testament used *porneia* to mean something different than adultery, the King James Version and numerous other translations translated Matthew's exception clause to refer to pre-nuptial sin, not adultery, Jesus told his listeners in Luke 16:18 that a woman whose husband had committed adultery could not remarry, the Greek underlying the exception clause matched the Septuagint Old Testament's underlying Greek for pre-nuptial sin in Deuteronomy 22:13-21, there was a logical theological explanation in favor of the Fornication View based upon the idea of covenant, the Fornication View could be seen in natural law, there were answers to the common objections made against the Fornication View that made sense, there had been Christians in every century after Jesus' who had rejected the Adultery View, and there were six clear places in the New Testament which discussed divorce and remarriage and which left no room for adultery being an exception. When faced with such compelling evidence, I had no choice but to abandon the doctrine which I had once so strongly believed in and embrace what God and logic were telling me. I believe that many of the people who will read this book will find themselves faced with that same decision. It is easy to stay where we are most comfortable. If, like myself, you have preached the Adultery View for years it can be very uncomfortable to make the change. But the truth is we have to go with where the evidence leads us. And if that evidence suggests that we have misunderstood something which Jesus taught we are compelled to not only reverse our understanding of it, but also to help others who have misunderstood it.

It is unfortunate that so many have become mistaken upon the one exception that Jesus gave but the best scholarship and all of the evidence brought together suggests that his only permission for putting away one's wife and remarrying was in the case of concealed pre-marital unchastity, a condition so important in the ancient world but hardly given a thought in our ultra-promiscuous modern world.

I want to caution, however, that I do not intend this to be either *my* or *the* final word on this subject. There are still many questions that I have. One thing I have become convinced of though, is that the evidence points away from adultery being what Jesus was referring to and any who make the decision to either remarry or perform a remarriage for a person on the grounds of adultery are doing so on very shaky ground.

Many, after reading this book and realizing that the Fornication View makes much more sense than the Adultery View, will wonder if it is possible to actually strike a blow against the stronghold that the Adultery View has. History and experience says, Yes. Many Christians in the past rejected the Adultery View and many still do today. What is needed are men and women, like those reading this book, who will work in their denomination and church to help people find out that there is an alternative view. There are many people who would embrace the Fornication View had they only been taught it. Like myself, they have never heard of an alternate view nor been presented with the evidence that so strongly supports it and they just assume that what they have been taught is the only view that exists. Change can come, but it will not come without the diligent work of God's concerned children.

May this work ignite a fresh desire within the Evangelical Community to reexamine the teachings of Jesus concerning divorce and remarriage

Appendix 1

Some Personal Observations Upon Divorce
And Remarriage Within The Evangelical Church

As I neared the completion of this work I began to wonder if Evangelicals would really take a book on divorce and remarriage seriously. As the years have went by a large percentage of Evangelicals have not only adopted the Adultery and Pauline Privilege views but a whole host of other "loopholes" which seem to conveniently allow any and everyone to remarry *regardless* of the cause for their divorce:

- Were you divorced before you were saved? If so, "all things have become new" and you are free to remarry.
- Have you asked God to forgive you for your unscriptural divorce? If so, God will forgive you, wipe your slate clean, and allow you to get remarried.
- Have you sincerely repented of your unscriptural remarriage? If so, God will forgive you and allow you to stay in the new marriage (even if your first spouse wants you back).
- Does your remarriage fall into a category that Jesus classified as "adulterous"? If so, don't worry—the adultery only occurred the first time that you had intercourse. All other acts of intercourse in the new marriage are accepted and honored by God.

Even though Evangelicals officially say that they believe that there are Scriptural guidelines for who can and cannot remarry after a divorce, for all practical purposes, many do not believe in *any* prohibition regarding divorce and remarriage. Of course they will make statements such as "Marriage is for life", "Divorce is wrong", etc. but when it comes down to it they do not really put these standards into practice. It seems that as the years pass by so also does the conviction amongst Evangelicals that there really is such a thing as an *unscriptural marriage*.

Appendix 2

The Testimony Of The Liberal Churches Who Preceded The Evangelicals In Abandoning Jesus' Teachings On Divorce And Remarriage

If the Evangelical Church was the first group of Christians to disregard Jesus' teachings on divorce and remarriage we would be left to wonder where all of this will ultimately end. Fortunately for us, we don't have to wonder because a previous group of Christians did just that and the results were disastrous—*Every denomination that today accepts homosexual behavior began by first lowering their standards regarding divorce and remarriage*. Within a generation of lowering the standards on divorce and remarriage they were using the same arguments to lower their standards regarding homosexuality.

- In 1959 the Presbyterian Church In The United States (PCUS), a precursor to the Presbyterian Church (USA), decided to do away with the Westminster Confession Of Faith's restrictions on divorce and remarriage.[282] Nineteen years later the denomination published a position paper on homosexuality indicating the possibility that there were "positive contributions of homosexual persons to the ongoing life of the church" and that there were "homosexual persons who manifest the gifts of the Spirit".[283]
- In 1973 the Episcopal Church, which in times past had taken a conservative stance on the issue of divorce and remarriage, decided that it would allow anyone who had been given a divorce

---

[282] Jack Rogers, *Reading the Bible: The Presbyterian Way.* Paper presented at the 1998 Covenant Conference, November 6, 1998. Available online at http://www.covenantnetwork.org/sermon&papers/rogerstalk.html, accessed July 20, 2010. Jack Rogers, *Jesus, the Bible, and Homosexuality: Explode the Myths, Heal the Church* (Lousiville, KY: Westminster John Knox Press, 2009), p.43-44.

[283] *The Church And Homosexuality* (Louisville, KY: Office Of The General Assembly Of The United Presbyterian Church In The United States of America, 1978), p.42-43. Available online at http://oga.pcusa.org/publications/church-and-homosexuality.pdf, accessed September 29, 2011.

to remarry.[284] Thirty years later they were ordaining their first openly gay bishop.

- In 1976 the United Methodist Church decided that where a marriage could not be fixed there was *always* the right to a remarriage.[285] Twenty-nine years later the United Methodist Council of Bishops was releasing a pastoral letter indicating that homosexuality should not be viewed as a barrier to church membership.[286]

- In 1982 the Evangelical Lutheran Church In America (ELCA) decided upon a process by which persons who had been divorced could remarry with the church's blessing regardless of the grounds upon which it had occurred.[287] Twenty-seven years later the ELCA were voting to allow homosexuals to serve as ordained clergy.

Many Evangelicals will probably be skeptical that the acceptance of divorce and remarriage has led to the acceptance of homosexual behavior in these churches. To answer that skepticism one needs only look at some of the reasons that people give for accepting homosexual

---

[284] Jerome E Politzer, *A Form Of Godliness: An Analysis Of The Changes In Doctrine And Discipline In The 1979 Book Of Common Prayer* (Philadelphia, PA: The Prayer Book Society, 1987). Available online at http://www.episcopalnet.org/TRACTS/Politzer.html, accessed September 29, 2011. See also Kenneth E. North, *Holy Matrimony, Divorce, And Remarriage According To The Canons Of The Episcopal Church.* Available online at http://www.canonlaw.org/article_matrimony.htm, accessed September 29, 2011.

[285] *United Methodist Church Book Of Discipline* (Nashville, TN: Cokesbury, 1976), p.71.

[286] *A Pastoral Letter To The People Of The United Methodist Church From The Council of Bishops,* Nov. 2, 2005. Available online at http://archives.umc.org/interior.asp?mid=10171, accessed September 29, 2011.

[287] *Teachings And Practice On Marriage, Divorce And Remarriage, A Statement of The American Lutheran Church, 1980, Sec. 3:16.* Adopted Sept. 10, 1982, by the Eleventh General Convention of The American Lutheran Church as a statement of policy and practice for this church (GC82.10.104). Available online at http://www.elca.org/What-We-Believe/Social-Issues/Predecessor-Body-Statements/American-Lutheran-Church/Marriage-Divorce-and-Remarriage.aspx, accessed September 29, 2011.

behavior in the church and they will see that even the supporters of the gay lifestyle in the church acknowledge this.

In a 2004 article entitled *The Church And Homosexuality* featured in the *Journal Of Lutheran Ethics* John Wickham, a supporter of homosexual behavior in the church, noted that if Christians could change their mind about accepting Jesus' teachings on divorce and remarriage why couldn't they change their mind about accepting homosexual behavior:

> Even more compelling is that most Christians today accept divorce and remarriage in spite of Jesus' explicit judgment that it is adultery (Mt 19: 3-9). Presumably, Christians forgive and accept it because allowing a second or third chance is the loving thing to do. **If heterosexual Christians can forgive and accept adultery among their remarried brothers and sisters, it smells like hypocrisy to deny sexual companionship and even marriage to their gay brothers and sisters**. If heterosexual Christians can manage to get around Jesus' judgments, they certainly ought to be able to get around St Paul's.[288]

In preparation for their 2005 Church-wide Assembly the Evangelical Lutheran Church prepared a document entitled *The ELCA Studies on Sexuality: Three Resolutions For Consideration At The 2005 Churchwide Assembly*. It was basically a proposal for how the ELCA could integrate those practicing homosexuality into the life of their denomination. Those in favor of the proposal process indicated that the decision to reevaluate homosexual behavior was no different than the church's decision to reevaluate its stance on remarriage after a divorce:

> People holding this view [that homosexuality is not a choice] believe all language excluding gay and lesbian persons in committed relationships is unjust and should be removed. However, there can be support for this proposal for two reasons: (a) while the language of Vision and Expectations continues, there

---

[288] John Wickham, *The Church And Homosexuality* in *Journal Of Lutheran Ethics, Vol. 4, No. 8* (August 2004). Available online at http://www.elca.org/What-We-Believe/Social-Issues/Journal-of-Lutheran-Ethics/Issues/August-2004/The-Church-and-Homosexuality.aspx, accessed September 30, 2011.

would exist an avenue by which gay and lesbian persons in committed relationships may be called into the ministry of this church, and (b) **just as it took the Church and the world many years to understand other critical issues, such as the re-marriage of divorced people**, this process provides the opportunity for continued discernment of where the Holy Spirit is leading this church.[289]

In 2009 Jack Rogers, a Presbyterian theologian and supporter of homosexual behavior in the church, noted that the Presbyterian church's decision to change its stance on divorce and remarriage was the perfect analogy for the church changing its stance on homosexual behavior:

In the 1950's, both branches of American Presbyterianism took the remarkable step of revising the Westminster Confession of Faith on divorce and remarriage...The Presbyterian denominations had turned away from what they considered a legalistic approach to marriage and divorce based upon a literal interpretation of biblical and confessional texts. Now they cited the spirit and totality of Jesus' teaching as mandating a pastoral approach that allowed exceptions to previous rules...How is this relevant to granting equality to gay and lesbian members of our churches? **Jesus' words that divorce is equivalent to adultery are among the clearest statements on a moral issue in Scripture**...If we were to take literally Jesus' teaching on divorce, we would still not be accepting divorced and remarried people as office bearers in the church. Yet church law now asks that we take literally less clear statements regarding homosexual behavior. It is a double standard: current church law permits a pastoral approach concerning marriage and divorce for people who are heterosexual

---

[289] *Daily News Reports From The Evangelical Lutheran Church In America 2005 Churchwide Assembly in Orlando, Florida, August 8–14, 2005, Day Five ELCA Churchwide Assembly Friday, August 12, 2005*. Available online at http://www.lcna.org/news/news-archive?staticfile=archive%2F2005-08-08.htm, accessed October 1, 2011. See also *The ELCA Studies On Sexuality: Three Resolutions For Consideration At The 2005 Churchwide Assembly*. Available online at http://www.halfwaycreek.org/sexuality.pdf, accessed October 1, 2011.

and mandates a legalistic approach toward people who are homosexual.

We can learn from the way in which the Presbyterian churches, north and south, slowly shifted from the legalistic proof-texting to looking at Scripture through the lens of Jesus' life and ministry. Jesus did not set forth immutable laws to break people. Rather, he set forth an ideal toward which we all should strive—lifelong faithfulness in married relationships. **The ideal could apply to gay or lesbian couples as well as heterosexual couples**.[290]

Lewis B. Smedes (1921-2002) was an "evangelical" gay rights activist who, at the time of his death, was trying to lobby the Christian Reformed Church to embrace homosexual behavior. He suggested that since they had taken a more liberal approach to divorce and remarriage in the 1950's that they could (and should) also take a more liberal position on homosexual behavior.

I have gone on this long about my church's about face in its ministry to divorced and remarried people in order to set the stage for asking about its exclusion of another group of Christian people. I refer to homosexual people who trust in Christ as Savior and want to follow him as their Lord…**Does the church's dramatic move from the exclusion to the embrace of divorced and remarried Christians provide a precedent for an embrace of homosexual Christians** who live together in a committed partnership? My own answer to my own question is, Yes, it does seem to me that our embrace of divorced and remarried Christian people did indeed set a precedent for embracing Christian homosexuals who live together.[291]

If things do not change it will only be a matter of time before the Evangelical Church finds itself losing the battle to homosexual behavior

---

[290] Jack Rogers, *Jesus, the Bible, and Homosexuality: Explode the Myths, Heal the Church* (Lousiville, KY: Westminster John Knox Press, 2009), p.44.

[291] Lewis B. Smedes, *Like the Wideness of the Sea?* in *Perspectives Journal, 14* (May 1999).

just as it has largely lost the battle to divorce and remarriage. Already we are seeing the rise of organizations and individuals promoting the idea of "born again gays" (men and women who claim that they can be both born again and gay at the same time)[292] as well as high profile Evangelicals who themselves have engaged in homosexual behavior.[293] Likewise, recent surveys indicate a growing acceptance of homosexual behavior amongst Evangelicals. A 2011 survey conducted by the Washington-based *Public Religion Research Institute* discovered that 44% of Evangelicals between the ages of 18 and 29 favor allowing gays and lesbians to marry.[294] When it comes time for the current generation of Evangelical leaders to step down and the younger, pro-homosexual Evangelicals to take over where will the Evangelical church end up?

---

[292] See such pro-homosexual and "Evangelical" organizations as: "Evangelicals Concerned" www.ecwr.org, "the Evangelical Network" www.t-e-n.org, "Christian Gays" www.christiangays.com, "Born Again Lesbian Music" www.balmministries.net, "Gay Christian 101" www.gaychristian101.com, "Gay Christian Network" www.gaychristian.net, "Gay Christian Online" www.gaychristianonline.org, "Gay Christian Survivors" www.gaychristiansurvivors.com, the Affirming Pentecostal Church www.myapci.org, and the Fellowship Of Reconciling Pentecostals www.rpifellowship.com.

[293] Such as Ted Haggard (who engaged in homosexual behavior while president of the National Association Of Evangelicals) and contemporary Christian musicians Ray Boltz, Jennifer Knapp, and Kirk Talley.

[294] Public Religion Research Institute, *Generations at Odds: The Millennial Generation and the Future of Gay and Lesbian Rights, Aug 29, 2011.* Available online at http://publicreligion.org/research/2011/08/generations-at-odds/, accessed October 1, 2011.

Printed in Great Britain
by Amazon